Joseph Taylor grew up in a suburb of Baltimore and spent a good portion of his life in the same community. Joseph attended local schools and met his wife in that same community. Other than life experiences, he has no subsequent formal education. Joseph and his wife married at the age of 21, and they both anticipated a lifelong love affair. Most of his professional career was spent at one company (nearly 45 years). As of this writing they have two children… both are happily married; and Joseph and his wife remain very close with them. They also boast two grandchildren.

When he was in his 40s Joseph started to branch out into various volunteer opportunities. Before long he was on the 'board of directors' of several organizations. As he reaches 70 years, he remains very active in several organizations and is most proud to have been honored with formal community recognition on two occasions.

During an approximate 15-year time frame, Joseph suffered an unimaginable depression. (It's the basis of this book.) He has no idea how he was able to hide this from his friends, family, relatives and other acquaintances. More than once he thought about ending his life. No one knows that. Soon, Joseph and his wife will be married 50-years. His wife is a very private person and he doesn't want his family and friends to know the full weight of everything that he dealt with. He is better now and thinks she is too. He just wants to leave it alone for now. This is why he has written the book using a pseudo name. Writing this book… and re-living the worst time of his life has enabled him to somewhat get over it… and move forward. One day soon, he may actually acknowledge that he is a 'senior'.

Joseph Taylor

DIARY OF A BROKEN MAN

AUSTIN MACAULEY PUBLISHERS™
LONDON • CAMBRIDGE • NEW YORK • SHARJAH

Ordering Information
Quantity sales: Special discounts are available on quantity purchases by corporations, associations, and others. For details, contact the publisher at the address below.

Publisher's Cataloging-in-Publication data
Taylor, Joseph
Diary of a Broken Man

ISBN 9798886937558 (Paperback)
ISBN 9798886937565 (ePub e-book)

Library of Congress Control Number: 2023917051

www.austinmacauley.com/us

First Published 2024
Austin Macauley Publishers LLC
40 Wall Street, 33rd Floor, Suite 3302
New York, NY 10005
USA

mail-usa@austinmacauley.com
+1 (646) 5125767

This is a work of non-fiction. The author would prefer that none of his friends or family members read or know of this book. The writings in this book are absolutely the truth based on the author's life experiences. The diary entries are absolute. Some diary entries have been eliminated from the publication due to multiple redundant entries/thoughts. This book was written under a pseudo-name.

Some Background Information

1970

I met my wife, Yohan (pet nickname), during our senior year at high school. We were assigned as driving partners in the Driver's Education class. Within a few weeks, she asked me to the 'Welcome Back' dance at the school. I was elated. As the date approached, I stressed on what to wear, how to act, what would her family think of me (we were both 16). I walked to her house and knocked on the front door. Her stepmother answered, and asked me to have a seat and indicated that she will be out shortly. She stepped away, and Yohan's sister entered the room. I supposed she's about four years old…a little butter-ball, very cute with dimples as she just stared and smiled…I nervously said, "Hi, what's your name."

No answer.

Yohan came into the room and we left to walk to the high school. We had a nice time, and this was the beginning of a four-and-a-half-year courtship.

In the weeks to follow, we often got together on Saturdays. I was informed to not use the front door, instead use the side door. Also, I was not allowed in the living room, I'd have to wait in the kitchen until she finished her chores.

I'd met one of her brothers. Many times, as I waited in the kitchen, he'd be washing the kitchen windows and/or washing and buffing the kitchen floor. Her stepmother would inspect them, and he'd often have to do them again…because it wasn't good enough the first time. This brother was 12 years old when I met him. When I'd ask Yohan about this, she told me that every day, her job in the morning, was to clean the bathroom, put a load of wash in the washer and then hang the clothes out to dry. Then after school, take the clothes from the clothes line, fold them and iron some of them. It was also her job to fix dinner or at least start dinner. She was in charge of getting her younger sister (half-sister), ready for bed…giving her a bath, changing clothes, reading a story etc. On weekends the entire house had to be cleaned, and it had to be perfect.

I learned that Yohan's birth mother died suddenly when Yohan was in the 2nd grade. She has a brother that is a year older than her and a brother that is four years younger than her. Within a year of her mom's death, her father briefly dated then married stepmother. In less than a year, her half-sister was born. I didn't realize at the time, that this tremendous change in her family dynamic could have been severely traumatic for her and her siblings in their future endeavors and relationships. During most of our dating years, her father barely spoke to me. If I said hello to him, he might or might not grunt a few syllables. Generally speaking, I was a very friendly person back then (still am), but as time went on, his presence became very intimidating to me…I found myself very nervous and unable to be myself in his presence. This continued for the many decades that I knew him. (So, I never really got to know him nor him know me.)

Eight months after we met, we graduated from high school together. Her family was invited to my graduation party, and my family was invited to hers. I felt the meeting of our parents was rather awkward. Her parents just are not friendly people. We both found employment soon after our graduation, and of course continued to date. Many dates were just spent at her grandparents' home or my parents' home. Even after eight months of schooling and weekend dates, we both agreed on how painfully naïve we both were. It was a couple of years before we talked about marriage, but we did agree that we'd save a wedding night for that first intimacy.

1972

At my parents', we'd often sit in the main living room, while the rest of my family was downstairs in the family room. As we sat on the sofa, she allowed me to touch her breasts and even kiss them. Yohan made a habit of wearing a bra that opened from the front, as I had problems in un-hooking one from the back. One evening, as we were sitting there, I was holding her and kissing her neck. Yohan had her hand off centered at my stomach with two fingers just barely inside my waistband. As she slowly moved her hand across my belly, those two fingers brushed across the head of my penis. She immediately pulled her hand back and apologized, saying that she had no idea that 'it' would be at the top of my pants. The head of my penis was wet, so she rubbed her fingers on the leg of my pants. I was in sheer ecstasy at this first touch. But she was totally embarrassed by this and she absolutely did not intend to touch me. I assured her that it was okay, and that if she wouldn't mind, I'd like her to touch me a bit more. She hesitated, but said yes, she'd like that. I unsnapped my pants, and pulled down the zipper. The head of my penis was poking out beyond the top of my underwear. She reached into my underwear and stroked the first few inches of my penis, then wrapped her hand around its girth. I didn't know what she thought of the wetness, but I didn't want her to think it was pee, so I told her it was pre-cum…natural lubrication. (Remember, I mentioned that we were both very naive?) At this 'first touch,' she did not go all the way down to my balls…after all; my family was just footsteps away. She said that she had no idea that 'it' would be so big…I wondered if she wondered how that thing would go inside of her.

Of course, going forward, we continued that sort of fondling. A few months later, we spent a Sunday afternoon having dinner with Yohan's grandparents (paternal grandparents) and even watched a bit of TV with them. They were very friendly towards me. I actually believed that I had a very good relationship with them. I felt so good about this relationship. When I overheard some conversation about re-painting the kitchen, I actually offered to repaint the kitchen, and eventually re-painted the entire downstairs of their modest bungalow. I was a good painter, and actually enjoyed doing it. Anyway, as the afternoon became evening, I drove Yohan back to her house. Her parents were not home, they had gone to visit the stepmother's family (about a three-hour drive). Yohan invited me to stay for a while, even though we were not allowed to be alone in their home, and I especially was not allowed in the living room. So, we broke the law and went into the living room and sat on the sofa. We didn't turn any lights on; however the room was partially lit from the kitchen fixture. So, the petting began. In no time at all, her hands were in my pants and my hands were at her waist. Until now I had not touched her that way. She shifted to allow me to touch a bit further. As I reached beyond her belly, I was totally surprised to feel her public hair…I just didn't think that woman had public hair (remember…naive). I too, then shifted to allow her touch to go further…all of this shifting and struggling…so I stood up. Yohan pulled my pants and underwear to the floor. As I stood with my clothes at my feet, this was the first time that I stood before her in all my glory. My throbbing dick was at her face as she remained seated on the sofa. As I looked down, I saw as thin shimmering thread of pre-cum trailing below me. She reached forward to cup my balls then slowly leaned in and kissed the head of my dick. At that very instant, headlights turned into the driveway and lit up the living room's sheer curtains. We composed ourselves in seconds and hurried to sit in kitchen chairs. When they entered the kitchen door, Yohan announced that we just came in from visiting the grandparents. I greeted them with a hello, and announced that I was just leaving. They didn't answer either of us. Her parents/family walked around us as I struggled to pass them to exit the same door that they entered. I would not be surprised if they felt the hood of my car…just to see if it was warm. (It would have been warm…we were only inside for about ten or fifteen minutes.) There's no way that they could have known that we were in the living room. However, it could be possible that I may have left a drop of DNA on the living room hardwood floor. As I got in my car, started it then put it in reverse, before backing out of the driveway, I pressed my hand against the front of my pants. I instantly ejaculated inside my pants. It seemed to last for at least 10 or 15 seconds. I've never had an ejaculate feel so intense.

Within five minutes I arrived at my house. Before getting out of the car, I inspected my 'damage.' My underwear was soaked, the bottom of my shirt had cum on it, and a large wet spot had seeped through my pants. Our house is a row home. Often, when returning home in the evening, it's not likely that you'll find a parking space close to your house. This evening I had to park about a dozen houses away…I hoped I wouldn't encounter a neighbor as I walked home with a large wet area on the front of my pants. (I didn't.) When I entered my front door, I went immediately upstairs to shower and change into PJs. I hung my wet items in my closet to dry…before putting them into the clothes hamper a day later.

1974

We announced our engagement in February and began planning our wedding for April of 1975. During our dating years, I'd met most of Yohan's relatives and close cousins. I felt as though I had a very good connection with everyone. However, my father-in-law to be was not speaking to me at all…and often berated Yohan. He had her really upset when he started threatening that he may not attend the wedding (but he did attend as well as pay for most of it). I and my family did pay for some expenses as well. Yohan had become quite a seamstress and insisted on making her own wedding dress. It was absolutely beautiful. I found out years later that as she and her father stood in the back of the church, he was trying to convince her that it's still not too late to call off the entire thing.

1975

We were married in the spring and married life was good. I was working full-time at a night-shift position, and Yohan continued her career in cosmetology. We rented an apartment for our first year and a half. It was one-bedroom abode in an older complex. Rent was $125.00 monthly which included utilities. We had fun choosing and buying furniture and various apportions for our new space. Our neighbors were seniors, and we established friendships with them that lasted for years. (Ray lived next-door to us and Marie was our upstairs neighbor.) Within a few months of moving in, we (separately) invited each set of our parents over for a dinner to show our space and show off our accomplishments. Both of those dinner dates turned out to be very nice.

During this first year of marriage, we did take a weekend trip that was most memorable for me. We decided to hit the road on a Friday after work, and go to Ocean City. At about 6:00 pm we packed our bags and headed out on a warm September evening. We planned on stopping at a mid-point to have dinner out. About an hour into the drive, Yohan slipped her fingers up the leg of my shorts. Those fingers found my 'junk.' She played with me a little while I was driving. Within a few minutes, she unsnapped and unzipped my shorts, and pulled my dick out of its underwear. She went down on me for about 10 or 15 minutes. I realized that if a trucker or bus passed us…they could see what was happening. I just couldn't believe how wonderful this entire experience was. I would not have guessed in 100 years that I could be so lucky, so happy at this moment. As my excitement grew, I realized that I was 'stretching out' in ecstasy. A glance at my speedometer indicated about 70 mph. I didn't say a word, but I did ease off of the gas pedal to around 50 mph. (Much more acceptable.) So those few minutes ended and she tucked me back into place. A few minutes later, we pulled into a shopping area and stopped for dinner.

After dinner, we both wanted to use the restroom before continuing the drive. There was a waiting line for the ladies' room and Yohan said that she'll just meet me at the car in a few minutes. When I got in the car, I took off my shorts and underwear and sat there with my erection. When she joined me, I laughed and said that I was ready for round two. She grinned and announced that there is no round two (I didn't really expect it…I was kinda just teasing about the whole experience). I got dressed and we continued our drive and had a wonderful weekend.

1976

We bought a small house that boasted two bathrooms and four tiny bedrooms. The house didn't show very well and it was clear that it needed a lot of TLC. I guess we didn't realize it at the time, but I'd now say it was definitely a handyman's special. The total cost was $27,500 and our mortgage payments were $325.00 a month (which included taxes and interest). Our parents thought we were in over our head…but we managed just fine. We visited my family and her family just about every week. As we needed advice and help with our 'new' home, her father did assist with some projects, and my father helped with painting the interior. One of the first projects we did was to build a deck onto the back of the house. We outfitted it with a picnic table, a wicker lounge chair and a porch swing.

During the warm evenings of summer, we would occasionally use that porch swing for intimate rendezvous. Our space was somewhat private, but not totally. There was a sense of risk that made these encounters so exciting. During the cooler months of fall we'd still use that porch swing to enjoy a few escapades but under the coziness of a warm blanket. Sometimes even the wicker chair became a 'place to remember.' Life was just so good.

With our house looking 'better' we wanted to start our family. Unfortunately, the start of our family was delayed as we suffered two miscarriages.

1980

I was still working nights, and Yohan was a switchboard operator at a department store. When she became pregnant, she could work for a while, but eventually needed partial bed-rest, so she had to leave that position. Our first child was born and we experienced parenthood during this year. Yohan took on various career choices over a span of several years including retail, floral design, bridal consultant, banking and eventually warehousing. I didn't know until years later that her ultimate desire after high school was to attend college to get a doctorate becoming a pharmacist.

Her father would not allow this… "Since that is not what girls do." I felt sorry for her when I learned of this. She had been a 'straight-A student' throughout her entire 12 years of school. She really deserved a chance to pursue the career she dreamed of. She likely could have been awarded scholarships to help pay for further education.

1985

I think the many different career opportunities were good for her, but I also believe it took a toll on her. There was an inconsistency and uncertainty. I wondered if she was experiencing depression. She refused to talk to me about it. We had our 2nd child during this period. In the months and years to follow (I feel really guilty about this but…) I was feeling neglected. Sex was sometimes months apart, and she refused to even accept any comfort from me. Every evening she would sit and crochet. She seemed to lose interest in me and in sex altogether. From time to time, I would ask her about this…but she absolutely would not talk about it. We'd only been married for ten years. Was this the end of 'good times?' Or is this just a lull that others experience as well? There was one evening where she was on the phone for a very long time. The other person seemed to be doing most of the talking…Yohan would only utter a chuckle or maybe an agreement from time to time. I was thinking about the lack of sex. So, I left the room, then returned naked and ready. I whispered, "Who ya talking too?"

She placed her hand over the receiver and said, "Rosie…I'll be upstairs in just a minute."

I said, "Okay" then as I leaned in to kiss her forehead, I clearly heard a man's voice on the other end…AND I recognized it. It most definitely was her friend, David. He has a slow 'hillbilly drawl' that is unmistakable. I'd met him before at a 'Container Party' whereas business comrades get together at a local bar, to consider business deals and relationships. He was one of those people that if he was talking with you…he would not look at you. I had a bad vibe about him on that first meeting. At this point, I went upstairs, lost my desire. It was a long time before she joined me…I pretended to be sleeping. I never told her that I knew she lied to me. I've re-played this in my mind many times.

1987

Our house needs so much, so we considered looking at new homes that were being built not too far away. We put our house up for sale and put a deposit on a new one. The new homes are very close to a popular public beach…This is what partially prompted our move to this particular development. We had never gone to that beach before, and decided to give it a try. One of our parents watched our kids as we left for our date. We packed a picnic lunch, brought blankets, towels and suntan lotion. As we arrived, we staked out our spot…and sat on the beach to observe and admire the space. There were many families there with their kids. Eventually we waded out into the water. We found that you could venture out pretty far and the water was still just over waist deep. We looked at one another rather liking our situation and enjoying the water on this summer 'date day.' she reached over and tugged at my bathing suit. I was hard in an instant, and a few moments later, she had my bathing suit in one hand and my dick in the other. As I stood in the water naked and loving life, she announced that if she ran up to the beach right now, I'd have no choice but to stay naked where I was…because I certainly couldn't run naked to follow her. She teased me for a bit about it…and I loved it. Of course, a bit later, I put the suit back on and we returned to the beach. It's one of many favorite memories that I'll always cherish.

After a year with no serious bites on our house, we took down the *For Sale* sign and chose to have our home totally, professionally remodeled. We spent $60,000 for this initiative. This would be the first of many re-finances or 'equity' loans that we would apply against our mortgage.

2000

Our relationship has been okay…I just wish it was better. This spring we'll be married 25 years. I'd been secretly saving money for quite some time and booked a cruise for our anniversary in April. Our kids would be old enough to be left at home (15 & 20). I surprised her with our tickets in January. I wanted to give her plenty of time to ensure she could take off from work as well as plan her wardrobe and all that other cruise 'stuff'. She was totally surprised and absolutely elated. This seven-day get away was PERFECT. We had the best time ever. And the sex was SO AMAZING. We just seemed to re-connect in a way that I never thought would happen. she engaged me so many times…She even coaxed me to have sex outside (behind some shrubbery…with people walking by). But I was so scared that we'd be caught, arrested and jailed in a foreign country…that I could not perform (but I wanted to, I wanted to). We laughed about that later, and Yohan even told this to some of my co-workers, just to tease me…we enjoyed the laughs all around. So, at this point, with our kids getting older, and this re-connection that we seemed to experience, EVERYTHING was coming up roses. I was anticipating that our second 25 years would be the best years of our lives.

2001

I've had my job for about 30 years at this point. Much of that time was evening and night shifts. At about this time I was accepting a nine-to-five position. Yohan was supportive, and I was touched when she sent a planter to my office on my first day. It was a good feeling that I'll always remember. So, I finally thought I could spend more evenings at home with our family. Yohan started, once again, working 60 hours with no incentive benefits to her pay…It seems like she just doesn't want to spend time with me. Later, she told me that she feared that she'll never have an evening to herself again (so that really brought me down).

On January 2, 2001, she was injured during an accident at the warehouse where she worked. Apparently a forklift driver did not see her standing with her back to him. He stopped suddenly, and part of the load that he was moving shifted forward and hit the back of her left leg and heel. It was close to the end of her workday, and she called me at work to pick her up and take her to the hospital. When I arrived, she could barely take steps to get to the car. Clearly, she was in lots of pain. At the hospital, we found there were no bones broken but there was internal damage and bruising. The doctor suggested that she take some time off from work to give this time to heal…A pain prescription was ordered, as well as a 'boot' to be worn. (*What we did not know at this time was that the injury would be life-long, and damage to internal tissues and nerves was permanent. A diagnosis was several months in the making. Within a few weeks, she would be attending appointments five-days a week. (Pain management, acupuncture, physical therapy, mental therapy and doctor appts.) She wore the boot for several months, and then went to crutches and eventually a cane. Her limp was pronounced and the swelling never went down. Never. The appointments lasted for well over a year. Eventually she also had two hospital stays for nerve conduction as well as a saddle-block to gage options for pain.*)

When we got back home from the hospital, she was exhausted and hurting…and didn't sleep well at all. She was in so much pain, that she could not allow the blanket to touch her. Believe it or not, she went to work the next day. I begged her to take time off but she refused. So, she went to work and kept her foot propped up on a chair. Co-workers got her coffee, water etc. As time went on, she refused to admit that she was down… (but I knew she was). I asked her to tell the doctor of my concerns. But nothing seemed to change. I'm sure she didn't tell the doctor any of my concerns, and she did not want me to talk to him. I asked her if it would be okay if I write a letter to him to voice my concerns…she said, "I guess so." I wrote a two-page letter and gave Yohan a copy. I let the doctor know that she also had a copy. After that letter, she was slowly weaned off of certain anti-depressants. I didn't know it at the time, but her doctor's report indicated that she was suicidal. I found this out several years later when she finally allowed me to read the doctor's reports on her.

After a few months, she did seem better in some respects. I knew she really liked her job, but I also knew she was exhausted. One day, when she got home from 12-hour workday, she actually fell asleep in her chair while holding a cup of tea. Most things in the home life had been okay for several years; two very level-headed kids, both had been assigned to honors programs at school. There had been music lessons, boy scouts, girl scouts, explorers club, a nice home, two cars, and she's an AVON lady too. But once again, there's still no time for me. I do a lot for my family and our community, and I just don't understand why she won't talk about us. I feel so underappreciated and neglected. (I know…I do feel guilty about this after everything that she's been through. But my feelings are real.)

2002

In November of 2002, it's now been nearly 2 years since that injury. Yohan was approaching a milestone 10-year anniversary at her job. There was a celebration at the office. The company provided lunch and she was given a huge vase of flowers. A week later she was terminated. *(We found later that when an injury occurs at a workplace, it's commonplace that the company will choose to not have that employee continue to work there…because of threats of lawsuits etc.).* she called me, told me she was fired…She was now just driving aimlessly. I asked her to please drive home I'd meet her. I was in a panic as I left work…that job was important to her. When I arrived home, we hugged and I kissed her forehead. We talked for about a half hour, and then I suggested that we go out for dinner. She hesitated because she was only getting one more paycheck. So we went to dinner anyway, then on a brief shopping spree…I thought it was important to just do that. We spent about $100.00 on bathroom accessories. Silly, isn't it? But I think it felt good for me and her. The next day she filed for unemployment (eventually denied because the injury that she's dealing with invalidates unemployment). I don't know how she did it, but soon thereafter she found part-time work where the management would allow her to keep those daily appointments in mid-afternoon, and then come back into the office. I have no idea how she manages to go to appointments five days a week for over a year…I know I'd go crazy. And I know she's depressed. Eventually, she changed jobs several times. Her depression seems to be getting worse. She doesn't laugh or smile. When we visit her family, she barely speaks. Her father has been having some health issues, and she doesn't even ask, "How are you doing?" It's crazy but it seems that I carry the conversations. It's not just there…it's everywhere we go. I've tried to talk to her about this, but she doesn't understand my concern, instead she thinks I'm complaining about her. I was very worried about her physical and mental condition, and I'm thinking that her condition may be quite complex with multiple contributing factors. Every couple of months I ask her about us and our relationship. She just won't answer.

Her only comment is to ask, "What are you doing, counting the weeks?"

I respond, "No, I'm counting the months." Am I making our relationship worse…because I'm asking her to talk about us? As God is my witness, I have no idea why we're in this unending purgatory.

November 20, 2002 (Wednesday)

I guess I still didn't learn. It's been close to two years with no sex, no slow kiss, no tender touch, no warm embrace, not even an "I love you." And, not so long ago, I thought we'd be entering the best segment of our lives. So, when we went to bed, I approached the subject one last time. I asked her if we could just please talk about our relationship.

She hesitated, then turned to me and slowly said with a huff in her voice these exact words, "Look, I don't love you, I've never loved you and I only married you to get out of that house." The cry that came from me…I'd never heard before…and I couldn't stop. Our daughter ran into our room.

"What happened?"

I said, "Your mother just told me she doesn't love me and never has."

She got on our bed, got between us and stretched out her arms to embrace us both. She was crying and I couldn't stop. As far as I could remember, Yohan was stoic. No emotion whatsoever. I don't know how long that scene lasted. My life had just ended.

I got dressed and went outside for a walk…I know it was after midnight, but I really didn't have a sense of time at that point. I walked for hours and cried until I just couldn't cry any longer. It was a chilly night so I hardly saw another soul. As the morning began to dawn, I thought I should go back home (they might be worried). I passed by the apartment complex where we lived at the start of our marriage. I went to our 'old address'…it appeared that the unit had been on fire, and there was some reconstruction happening (I could look in the window). This gave me an idea that I'll mention a bit later in these pages. When I got home, they were glad I was okay…and they were worried. I lay down on the sofa and basically stayed there for the next 10 days or so. I didn't go to work, I only picked at a few morsels of food and I barely slept. I didn't want to see anyone or talk to anyone. Later that afternoon, I turned on the computer and composed the following letter:

To all organizations that I have been part of:

Dear Friends,

It has been my pleasure to work with, and get to know each of you over these past years and in some cases over these past few weeks. However, due to severe personal trauma, I find that I must step aside and/or resign my positions in all organizations. My decision has been quick and it is final. I wish everyone continued success as you embark on a new year.

For those organizations where I have a commitment between now and the end of the year, I will honor those obligations. (Christmas party, Christmas parade, Christmas caroling.)

I sent this letter to five organizations. I just could not bear to talk to anyone about what I'd just experienced. When I returned to work, everyone was under the impression that I had been sick and just not feeling well. I told no one anything. It was hard to put on a happy face at work…and laugh when I was supposed to. I found that I was able to get away with doing as little as possible…which was not my true persona. My drive time to and from work was spent in uncontrollable tears. I parked on the top level so I could try to put on a good face before stepping into the office. Outside of work, I avoided everyone, everyone.

Our Old Apartment

After seeing our old apartment in November, I had this idea of a romantic dinner inside just for Yohan and me. During those 10 days on the sofa, I did venture out a bit, mainly for walks in the park. I went to the apartment complex and asked about the possibility of renting our old apartment for just a few hours before a new tenant leases it. I indicated that I'd like to take in a card table, 2 folding chairs and dinnerware…And that I would pick up carryout dinners from a local restaurant. The manager said she had no idea when our specific apartment might be available since it actually had been damaged in a fire. She had no timetable for the re-construction that was taking place. In addition, she was very reluctant to consider my idea. I offered $50.00 restaurant gift cards to a famous restaurant in our area…and I'd give those gift cards to everyone on staff (five associates). I told her I wanted to surprise my wife, and that she had really been through a lot in the last two years. She accepted my plan. I just had to wait until the apartment was ready.

About two months later, the apartment was ready. I purchased the five gift cards and turned them over to the apartment manager. She would give the key to one of the neighbors that she trusted…and she offered the neighbors address to me. (The neighbor lived just a few doors away in the same courtyard.) I met the neighbor, who kindly allowed me to deliver the card table, chairs etc. She allowed me to keep the key. When Yohan arrived home from work, I told her I had a surprise dinner for her. We left and drove to one of the restaurants that we often frequented. She started to get out…I said no, please wait here, THIS is not the surprise. I went inside and picked up the carry-out order. Then we drove just a few blocks to the apartment complex and parked the car. I told her that our dinner would be in our old apartment. She was surprised, but I was very nervous about this, my emotions were running very high. I had to make myself realize that this was not a fix-all for everything we've been through…and I could not expect miracles. But I did hope it would be a good first step to a better outcome.

We entered the apartment. I had the table prepared with a white tablecloth, flowers, candles and her grandmother's china. We opened our carry-out bag, and dinner began. Afterwards, we walked around the apartment (a tiny one-bedroom), and reminisced a bit. We recalled our old neighbors (likely long deceased). We knew Ray enjoyed listening to classical music on Saturdays, and Marie enjoyed cooking. They both kept our shared hallway and stairs immaculate. We recalled storing our bicycles in the bedroom. Privately, I reminisced (but didn't mention it) about our wedding night and how un-romantic it was. We were both excited and so exhausted at the time, and we had to leave very early in the morning to catch a plane. Our wedding night started and ended rather quickly. After checking the bathroom and kitchen we cleaned up our dinner items. I returned the key to that neighbor, and then we were on our way back home. I asked Yohan what she thought of the evening. She said it was "nice" and offered no additional comments.

March 2003

I was able to convince Yohan to try marriage counseling. She did not want to go. I pressured her and we eventually did agree to try it. Our insurance covered three sessions per year. So, we went. On each of our three sessions, we each spoke separately with the counsellor. Before our last session ended, we were called in together for a conversation with him. In so many words, he basically told her that if she wasn't careful, she could lose me…and that in fact he saw me to be a very good man. As strange as this sounds, I was horrified that he said those words. For sure, I know that she did not want to hear that. So…no progress from those sessions.

September 5, 2003 Fire/Flood (Friday)

I was at work, and would be staying a bit later than normal as I was virtually teaching a class that was on the west coast (I'm on the east coast). Since I was teaching, I also was not available to be reached by phone. When the class ended and I terminated the session…immediately my phone rang. It was a senior level management associate from my department (located in a different state). He said he was transferring a call from my neighbor. I was totally perplexed and for a few seconds thought, *who is this…is this a wrong number?* So the transfer happened and a woman's voice said, "Joe, this is Lisa, everybody is okay but your house is on fire."

I was confused and asked, "Who is this?" As I realized that the sequence of events was actually happening, another neighbor offered to come pick me up…since in my panic, it may not have been safe for me to drive. I nixed that offer and immediately left work and got into down-town traffic. I was shaking during the entire 40-minute drive. When I got into my neighburhood, my street was still blocked by fire/emergency equipment, and I parked my car about six or eight houses away. All I could look at was look at our house. The fire was out but the house seemed to be a total loss. A crowd was still gathered. I heard someone say, "There's Joe…go get his wife." (Yohan was in the home of the neighbor who called my workplace.) I didn't really see her dashing toward me…I was in a daze at the sight of our house.

She put her arms around me and said, "Oh Joe, I love you." *(Later, as we were recounting events, she said that she did not remember saying that. But you can't take that away from me, I know she said it. I didn't imagine it.)*

It was starting to get dark; the wind was picking up and a few sprinkles of rain had started to fall. Hurricane Isabel was due to hit our area by morning. Some relatives were among the crowd outside our house. A fireman told us to please be careful, because part of the first floor was now missing, but things were stable enough to go inside to see if there are any items of value that we might be able to salvage. Our living room and dining room were gone. Remnants of that furniture had been tossed outside. But as we walked through the kitchen, I glanced on the back porch, my heart swelled when I saw that one of the firemen had salvaged most of Yohan's heirloom china (from her birth mother and grandmother) and set it outside…prior to tossing out the china cabinet which was badly burned. In the face of all of this tragedy, I saw that as a remarkably kind gesture. Our relatives and a few others helped us go through the house and retrieve a few valuables. We filled the trunk of my car. Our insurance company has already spoken with us so we have a sense of what's to come (kinda). Its dark now, we're hungry, and need to find a hotel. We were invited to go to her parents' house for dinner. Aside from larger get-togethers at their house, this was the very first time that just we (Yohan, me and two adult kids) were invited to their house for dinner. We've been married for 28 years and their house is 10 minutes away. After dinner, our son returned to his house (about 20 minutes away) and our daughter, Yohan and I went to a local hotel.

Hurricane Isabel arrived during the evening. We heard from my son in the morning. His waterfront property and most of his street was totally flooded. We left our hotel room to join our son at his house. He had moved his vehicle to higher ground just in case a flood surge would happen. His basement was flooded up to the first-floor joists and his free-standing deck had floated away. He lost appliances, gaming equipment, furniture and everything else that was in his finished basement. There was going to be SO MUCH to be done in the weeks/months to come…but for the moment, there was nothing that we could do. A short time later, Yohan, I and both kids came back to the fire scene. We stood in the blackened kitchen, and I asked if we could just stop and say The Our Father (so we did) and ask for HIS blessings to help all of us get through this tragedy okay.

We moved to a different hotel where we stayed for about five weeks until we were able to rent an apartment. Aside from what we were wearing, we had no clothes. Our insurance company offered funds to take care of immediate needs. Our stay at the hotel was pleasant. Continental breakfast got old after a while, but the staff was so friendly. After staying there a week or so…they of course knew we were displaced. Some of them asked if we would be offended if they offered us used clothing. "Of course not," was our reply. They asked our clothing sizes. They planned on checking with their friends and families…any items that were offered they would put in our hotel room.

A few days later, we returned to our hotel room after work to find three bags of clothing. This kind action was repeated and repeated and repeated. Weeks later as we planned to move to an apartment, we had received (maybe 30-plus) bags of clothing. We kept EVERYTHING that we could use; items that were too large/small were taken to Goodwill. (But I needed to make three trips to Goodwill!) We sent three vases of flowers to the three organizers of the clothing drive. Their kindness still touches me every day. They have become part of who I am. As I type these pages nearly 20 years after that fire, I have purposefully kept one specific white shirt. It's a shirt that was offered to me in one of those bags by a kind stranger who I'll never know. I'll have to let someone know that I want to be wearing that shirt when I'm buried.

October 2003

We understood that the structure of our house was sturdy, but repairs and a rebuild of the entire interior would take about seven months. In the weeks to follow, we continued to receive an overwhelming outpouring of love and support. There was an organized effort in our entire neighborhood soliciting donated funds for our benefit. At my workplace, there were two separate efforts. One was from co-workers from my floor, and a second one was from co-workers in my department from different states, once again for funds. My parents and siblings (some from out of state) came together…and surprised us with additional funds during dinner at my parents' house. THEN my cousins/relatives invited us to celebrate a 50th birthday…but the party was actually for Yohan and me. It was like a wedding shower with gifts of cookware, bath items, gift cards, cash, and so many more gifts from about 25 people. Yohan & I were front and center in front of everyone opening gifts. Even as I write these words my eyes are glassy. Our friends at our local museum offered gifts as well. As overly generous and kind as these actions were, I did see a downside. No one at Yohan's workplace offered anything and none of her family or relatives offered anything. I felt just terrible about this. I know she was hurt. I don't recall that Yohan and I ever actually spoke about her family, work friends and relatives' inaction…but it's like the elephant in the room…we both knew it and we both felt the hurt.

January 2004

It's a new year and our health insurance will now allow three additional marriage-counseling sessions…and I've talked her into it again. We chose a different counselling office. During these sessions I've come to realize that she believes our relationship is passive/aggressive. This is the first time I've heard that…and I don't understand it at all. I believe that her depression has made her passive…remember when she wouldn't have conversation even with her own parents…and I felt like I was leading the conversations? Was she thinking that I was aggressive when so many times I would ask her about my concerns for her wellbeing? I just don't know. For the moment I accepted what she thought…just to appease her. But I really had no idea where she was coming from. By the end of our three sessions, this counselor basically gave us the same speech as the first one. This one also told Yohan that she's got a good husband. So much for that effort.

I wanted to find a third counselor and pay for the sessions…Yohan said she absolutely would not go to another counselor. She told me to go by myself.

I actually was wondering…after many, many opportunities to talk, she would never open up to me. Why would I think for a minute that she would open up to a counselor? I have a feeling that she never really divulged what her feelings were. I think she really needed long-term counseling as well as be a willing participant. She definitely was not a willing participant in our six sessions.

I made an appointment with a third counselor just for me. When I arrived, no one was at the office. I stayed there for about a half hour…but no one came. The next day I received a phone call apologizing for a scheduling mishap…so I re-scheduled. Unbelievably, the counselor missed that appointment as well. I took that as a sign to give up on it. Actually, I was afraid that this counselor would likely suggest that I leave the marriage…and there's no way that I'd do that. Despite all of our issues, Yohan has maintained that she does not want a divorce.

I decided that I'm in a really bad place in my mind…and as much as I did not want to treat my depression with drugs, I made an appointment to talk to a doctor…before I'd do something drastic. I started on a low dose of Paxil. I confided my thoughts with a good friend and co-worker, but I didn't tell him of my problems. I knew he had issues with depression and wanted his thoughts. He warned against that particular drug, as for him it made him unable to ejaculate.

After a month or two I felt no different, and that dosage was increased. With this dosage increase, I felt weird. I found that even if I wanted to cry…I couldn't. Strange as it sounds, sometimes a cry felt good, but I physically could not cry. I also found my co-workers warning to be absolutely true. I was unable to cum. An erection was no problem, but a climax was impossible. Masturbation was the only sex I could have…so this small slice of enjoyment was no longer possible. After re-thinking everything, medication did not fix our problems; it just made me feel different. All of the marriage issues were still on the table so I stopped taking the drug.

2004

Our house is finished and we can move back home. I think we had a good time outfitting the house, picking out flooring, furniture, curtains etc. On our moving day some of our neighbors even offered house-warming gifts. We've been far, far more than just fortunate. We'll never be able to pay forward the amount of kindness we've received. I wish I could say that all of the kindness that we've received has offset the difficulties in our lives and in our marriage, but it just doesn't happen that way. I don't know how it's possible to be so happy yet so sad at the same time. I just don't know what to do. Is it even possible to get the marriage back on track? Don't get me wrong, it's not all bad. I think we mostly enjoy one another's company. We go places, we eat out often, and we like to shop, but there's still no hugs, no slow kisses, no embraces, absolutely no intimacy, and no expressions of love…just going through the calendar…ending one day and starting the next.

Actual Diary Entries

August 29, 2004 (Sunday)

We had dinner at Applebee's. Our conversation was very serious. I asked Yohan if she feels any different now about our relationship, there was a very long silence. Then I said, "I guess silence means no."

She corrected me and said, "Not really, the silence means I don't know."

I came to the realization that she really feels no different about me today—then she did in November 2002. After 20 months and all of our efforts, she doesn't know. I absolutely fell apart right in the restaurant. The waitress kept coming to the table—I had to ask her, tears in my eyes, face wet, to leave us alone for a while. She pointed out incidences where she thought I was getting mad or out of control. I just don't see it. We have different perceptions of the same events. I realized no matter how much I felt I was walking on eggshells; it just wasn't enough. In going back to my original request from 20 months ago, I asked her if she would like for me to leave the house for a while–to give her space so that she can better get in touch with herself without any influence from me. She didn't say yes or no but instead offered that maybe she could go back to her parents' for a while. I didn't like that idea. Couple of reasons: I thought her parents would not be a positive influence for her needs. And we both knew that both of her brothers had tumultuous experiences with their father and step-mother over their girlfriends/wives. It would have been a divorce in the making if she moved into that toxic environment. We agreed that I would look for a place. I felt very close to Yohan as we contemplated this subject…so in touch and at the same time so distant.

August 30, 2004 (Monday)

I've been on vacation from work—did some volunteer work last week. This week I'm looking for a place to live. I picked up our 'weekly community newspaper' and left a message for the first 'furnished room' ad that I saw. Fifteen minutes later, Ms. Goldberg returned my call. Fifteen minutes later I was at her house. She requires a $100.00 security deposit and $95.00 weekly ($30.00 more if you want food). I told her that I'd move in in a day or two. I left her house to have lunch with mom, dad, my sister and her son. (This had been planned last week). We went to Bennigan's and I just couldn't bear to say anything about my situation.

I saw Yohan that evening, after Curves, after 7:00 pm. We talked for a while and I fixed us a cup of tea. I told her tonight would be our last night together for a while. We both cried…We both hoped that this is a good move. I'm actually falling apart because of the lack of progress in 20 months, but at least it's a move with intentions and some kind of goal. If you love something, set it free—does that work here?

August 31, 2004 (Tuesday)

Stuffed some clothes in a trash bag and moved into the boarding house. Later in the evening, I went country line dancing with some neighbors, but didn't say a word—just too difficult to tell anyone. *(Yohan would meet us there after Curves.)* Over the course of the remainder of this week, I came home every morning while Yohan was at work, had breakfast and lunch and did a few things around the house. (Vacation week.) Each evening, I was sure to not be there when she got home (trying to give her space).

On Wednesday, I started to say something to our daughter. She got mad and said she didn't want to hear it. I was in the pool in a floating-chair; she was sitting on the deck. She ran into the house and called her brother. I guess I'll tell them both when they're ready to hear it.

September 4, 2004 (Saturday)

Didn't want to go home on Saturday—didn't know what to do or where to go. Thought it was important for Yohan to be home without me. I don't really know anyone at the boarding house. I'm not allowed to even have coffee. So, I left in the morning as if I had somewhere to go. I got in the car and didn't know what to do—I just drove. I didn't want to go anywhere local, not even for coffee. I didn't want to see anyone. I went to a McDonalds on Rt. 40. Then I roamed around in Home Depot for a while—looking for nothing. Finally, I decided to go to a local park. I remembered Yohan saying that she had gone there a few times to read and unwind. Teary and very upset, I parked on the lot and began to walk to the far end.

"Uncle Joe," I heard.

I turned to see my nephew. "What are you doing here?" he asked.

"Just to relax," I answered. He was there for a birthday party. What are the chances…just when I wanted to avoid everything? We parted and he returned to his party.

I continued to the far end of the park. I lay down on a picnic bench. As I looked upward at the trees (Somehow, I was seeing a parallel to a tree's lifecycle and the lifecycle of a person), I could see strength and weaknesses as the leaves would soon be falling. I thought of myself as a leaf on that tree) I went to my car to get a pad of paper and a pen and scribbled a few lines.

September beckons. Our union appears strong…
As golden hues overtake a hint of scarlet brilliance…
Outer edges, curling in crispness…
My purpose complete. Strength is draining…
An autumn breeze so gently caresses…
The hour is near. I've lost my grip…

I fall from grace, unaware of others…
Am I not alone?
I dance briefly on the meadow…
Before one final swirl of glory…
A thicket ends my performance…
The air is chilly now…
My last glance outward sees the beginning.

September 6, 2004 (Monday...Labor Day)

Labor Day weekend came and went. No picnics, no family, no fun, only despair. A very defining two-week vacation. Now I could actually use a vacation from work, but back to work tomorrow.

September 7, 2004 (Tuesday)

Back to work today. I tried to pass off my vacation as "no big deal." I don't think my friends could tell that anything was up. I can't really accept it myself. I just can't talk about it. Very difficult emotional day. Stopped home for a quick salad then went to the grocery store. Bought instant soup, tuna lunchables and apple juice. Briefly ran into Richard (from church). Wished that I hadn't seen anyone.

Wednesday: Managed to fine-tune an important presentation for tomorrow.

Thursday: Successfully presented it to 150 associates.

Friday: Completely lost.

September 11, 2004 (Saturday)

Again, I left the boarding house early as if I had somewhere to go. I'm dying to just relax on the sofa with a cup of coffee. I haven't really met anyone at the boarding house yet except Larry (handyman). Drove to McDonald's again, then to the park. Who would I have to see today? Soon after, I started to walk in the park I run into: Ms. Goldberg (my new landlady), her grandson and Larry... from the boarding house. I think God just doesn't want me

to be alone right now. I'm forced to have these encounters.
I sat down to write another poem.

The Defining Moment

In that brief moment,
When poignancy is so great…
That the least gesture…
Will be seen forever…
That a sincere whisper…
Will roar and never fall silent…
So great that a silent thought…
Will consume all others…
And a spoken phrase…
Will destroy a life.

September 12, 2004 (Sunday)

Met Yohan at church—later she had somewhere to go. She didn't elaborate…and I have a sense that I shouldn't ask. Wondered if she was meeting David again. I went to my parents'…told them what we were trying—Mom cried. I really didn't want to talk about anything, but it did feel good to unload some of it. Later I went to the grocery store again This time I ran into Gloria. Will this never end? Soon I may have to go to Glen Burnie to shop and eat just so I don't run into any friends.

September 18, 2004 (Saturday)

Awoke early, don't know what to do. It's raining. I can't stay at the boarding house. I don't know what to do. By

10:30 I'm driving aimlessly. Decided to take a trial run to Towson since I may have Jury Duty on Tuesday. However the beltway was backed up, so I took the next exit. Before I knew it, I spent two hours in Burlington Coat Factory and spent about $400.00 for stuff that I really didn't need—not even sure if I want the stuff. I bought a coat for Yohan. I threw everything in the trunk. Didn't speak with Yohan today; I really miss her. Cried in the car on the way back to the boarding house.

September 19, 2004 (Sunday)

Awoke early, showered, tried to kill time so as to arrive back home after 9:00 am. (Yohan goes to church extra early for a children's class…then mass afterwards.) Our daughter was still asleep…and wasn't going to church. I had some breakfast then met Yohan and our son at church. Mom and dad were there but she got cold and left early. My cousin was there, we met her boyfriend. We went to Yohan's parents after church. Our usual routine feels good after so much disruption. David was there (again). I never liked him and I don't trust him. David left about 10 minutes after we arrived, Yohan and her step mother followed him out to see him off. I don't think Yohan has ever followed someone out till now. I was certain they're talking about me. Inside, I was trying to tell Yohan's father about some bricks that were piled at a demolition site. (I knew the site owner and my father-in-law had previously asked me if I could get him the ok to take some bricks.) But I realized that he would not look at me and he pretended to not hear me. Instead, he kept rambling about some motor to our son. During our entire 30-minute visit, he would not look at me, so I just shut up.

The three of us went to a local fair…killed some time, walked around. Yohan had a $50.00 certificate for Macaroni Grill so we traveled to there for dinner. After dinner, we took a ride to Fort Howard to see the old 'boat-shaped house' that will soon be demolished. I asked our son to call his sister and set up a time so the three of us could have a conversation *(me and my two kids)*. Yohan and I went home—very long talk. Keeping my fingers crossed that we're on the same page. Gave her the coat and 'decorations box' from Burlington…then went to BH *(Boarding house)*.

September 21, 2004 (Tuesday)

Just can't go dancing. *(Yohan and I joined our neighbors and enjoyed country dancing every Tuesday for about 10 years…)* I don't want to see anyone. They might ask how things are going and I just can't handle it. I e-mail the neighbor to let her know I wasn't going this evening since I was fighting my own demons. (They know our situation.) I thanked her for being a good friend. Still, no one at work knows that I'm living in a room. My number wasn't called…so no jury duty. I decided to get my 'stuff' out of the trunk…having a very guilty feeling.

September 22, 2004 (Wednesday)

Went home after work. *(Yohan always gets home after 7:00 pm so it's convenient to stop and get something to eat…I leave before she arrives home.)* Not sure why I came home. Work treated to a huge lunch at Cheesecake Factory. Not planning on having dinner so I just went on ahead to the BH. But while I was home, I picked up a 'plaque' that had been on my dresser. I want to set it on my dresser at the BH. The kids had given this to me many years ago. It was just a piece of wood. They had printed their names on it: to daddy with a heart on it. Holding the plaque in my hands made me recall a few years ago, during a major thunder storm, our power went off, and our basement flooded with about six or eight inches of water. Later as Yohan and I sifted through the wet boxes to see what we could salvage; I filled with emotion and began crying in our basement when I found this 'plaque' floating in a box that also contained a wooden fruit bowl and fruit that we purchased on our honeymoon in Bermuda. I absolutely fell apart holding these items in my hands. Yohan was right there and displayed no emotions, no compassion.

Crying right now.

September 24, 2004 (Thursday)

Spoke with mom from work. Aunt Rosie passed away this morning. And Uncle John had heart bypass…and he's doing fine. Also spoke with Yohan from work…She says she has something important to talk to me about and that we'd talk later. I begged her to just tell me now. Turns out that I am no longer welcome in my in-laws' home. It felt like 1000 lbs. on my shoulders…I don't understand it at all. We stop at their house nearly every Sunday and have coffee and some conversation. After 30 years, why am I not welcome? Was very hurt by this, tears welling up. But I can't right now I have a class to teach in a few minutes. Went to my house after work to see if I have any flea-market messages. *(I am chairperson of the event.)* Also, the 1st Concert in the Park is tonight. *(I am corresponding secretary.)* I checked the mailbox…there's an invitation from Yohan's sister addressed to Yohan and family. I broke down. I've never been close with that part of her family…but we also never had an argument or anything. No one was home then. I called Yohan's sister and she exclaimed that she was told that I was 'out of the picture.' I went to the concert, but left during intermission…It's just way too difficult to see so many happy people while I am at the lowest point in my life. When I got back home, Yohan was waiting…we fixed a cup of tea and sat in the living room. She had not yet noticed the invitation…when she saw it, she was really upset. I told her I spoke with her sister…and now WAS invited. But I know I'm not welcome. I gave her a long embrace and a few kisses. I love you Yohan (but I couldn't say it). It hurts so much when she can't return the phrase.

I started to drive to the BH, but without even thinking about it…I got on the beltway and found myself going over the bridge. It was evening…I was not aware of what time it was or if there was any traffic out. I don't think there was traffic around, but I'm not sure. As I reached the top of the bridge, I slowed. I wasn't planning on jumping…I just wanted to see what the area looked like. I didn't quite come to a stop but I did take a long look. I was not crying. I had no thoughts of my wife, family, friends or anyone. Soon I was off of the bridge. Now I'm crying. I'm afraid to drive back over the bridge to return home. So, I managed to drive through the city to avoid getting on the bridge again. When I got to the BH, I went right to my room, cried half of the night. Surely, one of the worst days in my life. Have been saying prayers…need help…compassion…anything from Yohan. Just can't live like this.

September 25, 2004 (Friday)

A lot to do at work today…trying to get furniture donated to our community. Yohan and I exchanged a series of e-mails today. Kinda cute, I liked that. Yohan's sister called her… it sounds like the conversation between me and her sister was all misconstrued… her parents got involved… and I guess it's now a big thing. Her parents are worried sick about her. Once again, I agree with Yohan that it would not be worth it to have a conversation with her parents and family. (Kinda sad.) Even she says that as long as she and I are on the same page… that's all that counts. After work, I didn't know what to do or where to go. Often we would go out for dinner on Fridays. So, I went to Wendy's… got a piece of chicken…ate it on the Home Depot lot…in the far corner… hoped no one would see me. Then I walked around in Home Depot. Arrived at the BH by 6:30. Everything is quiet. I'm alone with my thoughts.

September 26, 2004 (Saturday)

There's a birthday party today for Yohan's father. Of course, I'm not welcomed. And on top of that, her younger brother is due to be there…he's in from Iraq. Surprisingly, her brother and his wife came to our house later in the day for a visit. So, I met his new wife and saw the many photos that he brought from Iraq. Both of my kids were there too. It was nice…and there was no mention of my in-laws. (Even better.)

September 27, 2004 (Sunday)

After church, I went to the grocery store…hoping that I wouldn't see anyone. I feel like I'm wearing a big sign on my chest saying, "I'm the cause of a failed marriage." But…I ran into two friends…hate this. My parents took me to dinner at Squires. We had a nice dinner and good conversation. From there we went to the funeral home. At the end of the day, I went back to my house for socks and underwear. Emotions kicked in and I felt sad about having to go back 'home' to the BH. I had to leave quickly.

September 28, 2004 (Tuesday)

Arrived at work early so that I could store my groceries in my office…without anyone noticing it. (Instant oatmeal, cream of wheat, tuna fish, cup o soups, potato chips). Have now lived at the BH for a month.

September 29, 2004 (Wednesday)

Covered the pool today after work. Hurried to eat a sandwich and leave before my wife gets home. As I was leaving, I realized that she has bowling tonight. Just want to make sure she has plenty of time without me. In my room by 7:00 pm.

September 30, 2004 (Thursday)

Average day, nothing special. I sent Yohan an e-mail kiss. She returned it! At the BH by 7:00 pm.

October 2, 2004 (Saturday)

Had to cancel today's flea-market due to rain in the morning. We were scheduled to go to the home of one of my co-workers today for a get-together for nine others that were laid-off. Yohan didn't want to go. I was hurt and disappointed…she's my other half. (But I couldn't say a word…just accepted it with a smile.)

October 3, 2004 (Sunday)

Today was the party at her sister's house. Yohan went alone. It was a very emotional day for me. I re-hashed "how could they write me off" so quickly. I guess I kinda poured my heart out to her before she left. I thought about this all day. Later, I thought that maybe I shouldn't have mentioned any of this this to her just before she was leaving. I sat on the porch swing and cried for about a half hour wondering if I did the wrong thing. Certainly, it was not planned or intentional to ruin her day. I realized that often when I have a serious conversation with Yohan her face falls so still— no emotion—no expression— no comments. I'm really starting to believe that she really doesn't love me and there's nothing that I can do.

October 5, 2004 (Tuesday)

Our last night for country dancing. We went…a few hugs with friends…exchanged various phone numbers. It was ok. As I was taking Yohan home, 'I Love You' by Climax Blues Band was on the car radio. Every song— every song peaks my emotion. It seems like just about everything I hear on the radio is speaking only to me. I filled up, but I don't think She noticed. I walked her to the door, and kissed her goodnight. She closed the door. She didn't even wait to watch me get to the car. I cried all the way to the BH.

October 9, 2004 (Saturday)

Community Flea Market today. Met Yohan at 6:30 am to go to the lot. At this flea market, her older brother and her sister were there. I'm not ready to deal with that sister yet after the 'invitation episode'…our eyes never met. Her brother's wife came later. I gave her a hug, we laughed a bit…I realized that myself, and two others who married into the family are all three hated by our in-laws. I kept that thought to myself. My daughter came with her boyfriend. I can't deal with him just now…too many negatives facing me right now. I gave Yohan a kiss in the morning—really do love her, really do want to spend the rest of my life with her.

October 10, 2004 (Sunday)

I met Yohan and our daughter at the church. Afterwards, I had tentative plans to go to a restaurant in Westminster. I invited them but ended up leaving the parking lot alone. A short time later they called and said they'd like to go. Hooray!!!

October 14, 2004 (Thursday)

My daughter has pulled a muscle in her back and will be out of work for a couple of days, so she and my son can meet me for dinner tomorrow night. I left home over six weeks ago and never fully explained why to the kids…so that's tomorrow. Have a lot to tell them and at the same time I don't know what to tell them. Haven't seen Yohan since Sunday but we've e-mailed a few times (I like that). I submitted a poem in a poetry contest a few weeks ago. They say I'm a finalist. And then want me to turn in another 'piece of work.' I asked Yohan yesterday for the 28th anniversary poem that I wrote. Did she still have it or was it lost in 'the fire.' She'll check. Well, she found it and put it on my file cabinet…I saw it when I got home from work today (to eat a quick salad). It was written 18 months ago and still so true today with no progress in all this time. Tears wet my face as I drove to the BH.

Love Endures:

Many years…Seems a few.
Broken hearts…Start anew.
Embers smoke…Flame ignites.
Love endures…I await.
Soars a dove…Free and yonder.
Clouded thoughts…Bid remember.
Return to nest…That has taken.

Granted not…Nor forsaken.
Flame ignites…Fire roars.
I await…Love endures.

October 15, 2004 (Friday)

My daughter called me at work to confirm that she and her brother would join me for dinner tonight. I had so much time to think about this. Well…here goes. I met them at home and suggested a restaurant. We went, ordered and I didn't know how to start. So, I said, "Okay now, what was it that you wanted to tell me?"

We had a brief chuckle, and then I went into everything. I think they understood. They didn't ask any questions. My daughter said almost nothing but she did fill up a few times. My son said he doesn't know what to say to neighbors, and they all are asking. I told him he could tell them anything…including the truth or he could just say he prefers to not talk about it. I have no secrets here. Later, he asked what would we do for Thanksgiving or Christmas since I wasn't allowed at 'the in-laws.' I said that I can't think about that right now it's too far ahead. At this point I'm not sure if I'll ever go to 'the in-laws' ever again…regardless if we get back together or not. My son asked me about being hurt vs mad at 'the in-laws.' I explained that after knowing them for 35 years, I can't believe that suddenly I am not welcomed. I didn't do anything…they had no problem just writing me off…without even asking me or Yohan. Yohan just told them a little of our situation and they just came to this decision. Then my sister-in-law omitted me from her party without even asking Yohan anything…nothing. I teared up at the table and we left. I had just paid the bill…I think they understand.

October 17, 2004 (Sunday)

Went to Baltimore Museum of Art (90th anniversary) with Yohan and our daughter. Had a nice afternoon. I was a little disappointed that Yohan visited her parents for such a long time before coming home to go to the museum. (I'm guessing that David was there. He's now there every Sunday…taking my place. This is a classic move by the in-laws…interfering in any way that they can to break up a marriage. We've already seen this type of drama with regard to both of her brothers. After going to the museum, we went to Ruby Tuesday's for dinner.

October 19, 2004 (Tuesday)

At work today did a presentation to about 85 people—wonderful…all went well. Boss called—says 'Best Ever.' One of my co-workers sent me a scripture today…it really hit home. I saved it and forwarded it to Yohan. I told her that I'm really going to try to pull myself out of this hole—based on this reading. I asked her to say a prayer for me for success. My neighbor offered dancing tonight at a new place, but I said no…I just don't feel like it. On the way home (BH), I stopped at Wendy's for a piece of chicken and a diet Coke. Then went to Home Depot and parked on the far end of the lot to eat it. As I was sitting there, I realized just how paranoid I'd become. Not a good thing…didn't want anyone to see me. I wondered how long I'd be doing this. She said I could come home anytime that I want to…but it's not about that. It's anytime she wants me to. She hasn't even said anything to indicate that she even misses me. At the BH sat on the front porch till nearly 8:00 pm…had three glasses of wine. I like the guys living here as well as the landlady and grandson. Guess I still can make friends pretty easily. Not sure if this is a good thing though. I never really drank this much beer or wine nearly every night. Enjoying it at the time…but questioning it later.

October 20, 2004 (Wednesday)

When I arrived at the BH today after work, I found a fellow boarder (Will) on the front steps crying. Said he just heard his sister died in a car accident today. She lived in Virginia. He talked about her for quite a while. When another boarder came home, they both disappeared for about five minutes…then Will returned. I have a feeling that something is up…they're into something. Will told me that Ms. Goldberg nearly put him out, and that she suspected drug use. He convinced her otherwise. He asked me if I had anything to do with it… (I didn't). The whole situation scares me a little. Drinking, smoking. What's next? I'm gullible right now…but these friends are making me feel better. I can actually laugh.

October 21, 2004 (Thursday)

Yohan e-mailed me today at the end of the day. She hasn't heard from me for a few days—am I OK? I said yes, I guess. Just trying to give her space. I'm kinda touched that she took the time to ask me though. She says that she may go to a fall festival on Saturday, could I be home for the washer delivery. Part of me is glad that she's making friends and developing interest. And part of me is sad because she's doing things that I really enjoy doing with her. I feel a bit left out.

October 22, 2004 (Friday)

Yohan is going to the fall fest with a friend from work tomorrow (I'm thinking David). She asked me to come home between 2:00 and 4:00 pm for the washer delivery. I don't know what to do till 2:00 pm…on the spur of the moment I went downtown. I made an appointment for a haircut the following week, then went to Federal Hill and sat on a bench for about a half hour. Then I went to Harbor Place and just strolled around. Spent $$ for cigars for the guys on the porch at BH. Walked all around. Had coffee and pastries at Starbucks. When I came back to near home, I went to the liquor store and bought a box of wine and vodka. Oh, and I had also spent $50.00 at Barnes and Noble. Once at home, neighbors were out front. I did talk to them a bit…One neighbor hugged me in the street a couple of times. Drank two martini's waiting for the washer. After the washer was delivered…I called a neighbor out back (dancing neighbors), and talked with her for a while. Back at the BH…wine, moonshine, snacks. In bed after midnight. Landlady invited me to join her for breakfast at 7:30 pm. Sounds GOOD.

October 23, 2004 (Saturday)

Yohan invited me for dinner after my 'Society Tea planning meeting' (pot roast). Daughter was home as well.

After dinner…some conversation. For the first time she said that she misses me in the evenings. It was like a beautiful song. Music to my ears. Maybe this will help me 'come around.'

October 25, 2004 (Monday)

Busy day at work. Landlady offered Beef Stew (perfect). Went to bed by 10:00 pm, but woke up at 2:00 am with a nightmare. A dark shadow with something shiny was attacking me as I walked a dark path at home to bring the trash can to the front. I woke up screaming "Yohan! Help me!" Eventually went back to sleep, then had a dream that the in-laws were putting me out. Never slept again that night.

October 31, 2004 (Halloween)

Usually I spend this evening outside talking with all of the neighbors, but I really didn't want to see any of them this year. Being paranoid again. Didn't want to talk to anyone who knows me. So I stayed at the BH. Landlady says she sits outside in a lawn chair. I asked if she'd mind if I joined her. Before I knew it, the other boarders joined as well. We all had a few cocktails…weren't too many kids out. I hung over the fence and talked to a few of those neighbors. When the time came to call it quits, landlady said let's go across the street (neighborhood bar)… And say trick or treat. This was my first time in this place, it was about half full. We laughed for at least an hour and a half. Then the landlady (64 years old) lifted her blouse for beads. I found out that she was a stripper on the block and made some really good money. She says she had lived it all, seen it all and done it all.

November 5, 2004 (Friday)

I didn't sleep at all last night…the boarder in the next room was acting crazy. After work I spent the entire evening at the BH. We sat on the porch, had a few beers, a few glasses of wine…probably not a good thing. That boarder was put out of the house in the morning. He trashed the room and peed on everything.

November 6, 2004 (Saturday)

They (landlady and two boarders), were all cleaning the trashed room by 7:00 am. I heard all of the activity…by 9:00 am I dragged out of my room. They were all laughing, joking. Before I knew it, I offered to clean the bathroom. Actually, I had nothing else to do anyway. Within a few minutes, they handed me my first glass of wine. I drank it, then another, then two beers—all while cleaning the bathroom. By noon we were all in the kitchen having eggs, toast scrapple, coffee. I had to leave by 2:00 pm to help set-up for the 'afternoon tea' event.

November 12, 2004 (Friday)

I had a difficult time focusing on anything at work. A lot of people took off for a four-day weekend. I daydreamed and wrote the following:

These last few years…Have seen much awry.
Nothings as it was…A part of me has died.
'Twas a short time ago…I had all I wanted.
As heartache and despair…Grip my soul.
I now have nothing…My desires thwarted.

As Christmas draws near…For that one Silent Night.
Send my gift to another…Influence their life.
What I truly desire…May never be.
For that which is so…Precious.
Must be found…Within me.

The next day, I showed this writing to Yohan. She wants to know what the last three lines are supposed to mean. *(It means that I want her, but have no idea how to reach her.)* I printed a few copies of this poem on 'Christmas Paper' letterhead. I gave copies to our kids and to Yohan. I really don't want any gifts…and don't want to give any. Once before (in good times), ask them to donate funds to organizations in my name instead of giving me gifts. I actually like that whole idea.

November 14, 2004 (Sunday)

Met Yohan at church. After church, she went to her parents' house. I encourage her to do so, and at the same time it hurts me very much. We had a wedding to go to today…we sat with our neighbors. Afterwards we came back to our house and talked for about an hour. I'm ready to come home, but I don't think she wants me to. I hope this whole thing wasn't a giant mistake. We talked about

Thanksgiving. Yohan's doing so much that hurts me in the name of recovery. I actually think she's not going to have dinner with me. I'm crying as I write this. I don't think I have the strength to go to a restaurant with my family and some relatives. I just can't join them without her. Not only does she not love me…I'm thinking that she despises me. When I returned to the BH, the boarders asked me to sit on the porch for a while. Before I knew it, the time was 12:30 am and I had about four beers. I gotta get out of here soon before I really fall off the deep end.

November 16, 2004 (Tuesday)

I'm ready to come home. Ready to be with Yohan and see what happens. Bad influences around me constantly. I could get wrapped up in it so easily, but so far I haven't. Alcohol and drugs are all around me…right in front of me…and quite available. Yohan says 'coming home' sounds good to her. I decided to come home on the first weekend of December. Was sooo happy all day! Really Happy. I stopped at the bakery and bought some turnovers, then went back to the BH. Sat on the porch w the landlady and told her I'd be leaving on December 3rd. She really hates to see me leave. A few minutes later she told me that two other boarders (brothers) are leaving soon too…She caught them smoking in the house…and they're having trouble paying their rent. I felt guilty…kinda hated to leave her.

November 18, 2004 (Thursday)

My boarding house friends are supposed to be leaving tomorrow, but they have no place to go. They are both 'jailbirds' (their words), but they are nice people. I think they could really use a break and some understanding. When I got back to the BH after work, I found all three of them on the front porch. Between us we finished a box of wine and a 12-pack. (This was their farewell party.) I went to bed at midnight…then up at 6 to go to work.

November 19, 2004 (Friday)

Up at 6:00 am—out at 7:00 am. Landlady and one of the borders (Larry), are on the front porch. She's holding a glass of wine. They're mad at me because I don't have a hangover. Last night I advised all of them to not burn your bridges and to remember that you travel a bridge two ways. After work Yohan and I were going out for dinner. We talked about my wish to not receive Christmas gifts. I just don't need or want anything…I'd prefer to give back. When I returned to the BH—the gangs all there. They worked out a solution. I sat on the front porch until midnight.

November 21, 2004 (Sunday)

After church, Yohan visited her parents. She told them that I'd be moving back home soon. They said that I'd still not be welcomed at their house. I think that they are just hateful, hateful people. I had words with Yohan regarding her loyalty to them in the face of my despair.

November 23, 2004 (Tuesday)

I was back at the BH by 8:30…and sat up till after midnight (again).

November 24, 2004 (Wednesday)

Called mom this morning. Broke my heart but had to tell her that I just can't go out for Thanksgiving Dinner without Yohan. She was very understanding and that made it easier for me. I told her that Yohan and I could stop over in the evening. We would bring a pie. I suggested to Yohan that I'll be staying home at our house all afternoon by myself. She suggested, "K-Mart is open today; walk around in the store for a bit." Once again, there's no compassion for me whatsoever. Guess I'll eat a hamburger for thanksgiving if McDonalds is open. Up till 12:30 am at the BH.

November 25, 2004 (Thanksgiving)

Once the crew at the BH realized that I'm not having dinner till sometime after 3:00 pm, they insisted that I stick around and have a bit of Thanksgiving with them. I didn't tell them that I actually had no plans for a dinner. Yohan and both of our kids were spending Thanksgiving at her parents' house for the first time EVER. They've never invited our family to join them for Thanksgiving until now. I didn't really want to stay at the BH either but I did for a while. Dinner was actually ready by 11:30. By 11:55 I had eaten…and left soon afterwards returning to my empty house. All I did was sit on the staircase with no TV, no fireplace, and no lights on. One of my neighbors must have realized that I was home alone. She left a message twice to invite me over…I didn't answer the phone. A short time later someone knocked on the door…I didn't answer (but I did appreciate their concern). I eventually met Yohan at my mother's house…then back at the BH by 8:00 pm.

Ms. Goldberg and Larry were on the front porch. They've got to be tired. Of course, I joined them—couple of glasses of wine. The evening was rather cold. We all sat under a quilt. It was ok. I guess I seemed down and they noticed. They wanted to set me up with a prostitute. REALLY! Ms. Goldberg had a $100.00 bill in her pocket…and I could have it…and she knew some good girls. I know that they meant well, but I found it disappointing that they'd think I'd do that. Even though Yohan doesn't love me and it seems that often she's intentionally hurting me…I still love her. God knows that I have not has sex for years at this point and I really need and want a sexual relationship…but it has to be with my wife. Overall, this was one of the saddest, most memorable days of my life. I'll never forget it. Oh yeah, on the porch till midnight again, drowning my sorrows.

December 3, 2004 (Friday)

Can't believe it's December. I'll be moving back to our home tomorrow morning. I stopped at Wendy's after work and had a bowl of Chili (and yes…still went to a distant parking lot to eat it). Sat in my room, reflection.

Evenings draw early as December looms…
This hopeless feeling as I dwell in my room…
Thanksgiving wrought sadness as families embraced…
Barter my life for a happier space.

Days cloudy and misty as December looms…
Er desperate thoughts foster my doom…
A light in the distance seems out of place…
Dear Lord, let it shine on my face…

A morning snow blankets as December croons…
Glistening with purity as a new day blooms…
A conscious decision captures my life…
Coddle the moment not taken is strife…

December 4, 2004 (Saturday)

Moved back home this morning. I got here at about 9:30 am. No one was home. I guess I expect too much. I thought at least someone would welcome me back. I fixed a huge breakfast, cleaned my mess then had lots to do today. This weekend is the annual Christmas Parade…I have to get our 'entry' put together, as well as our community Christmas Party is tomorrow…and I have lots to do. Yohan agreed to help with the many tasks. We completed everything, then by 9:00 pm we're exhausted. It felt funny sleeping with her.

December 10, 2004 (Friday)

Yohan's birthday is today, she'll turn *51*. Over the years, for different occasions, I've planned a few surprises, a few 'special' gifts…not the usual sweater or purse. I've written poetry several times…and planned special evenings (like the dinner at our apartment). It has occurred to me that the things I see as special…seem to be more special to me than to her. She has never commented on poetry that I've written for her. Of course later, if I asked what she thought about it she'd say, "It was nice."

Today, I don't have a gift. I'm off from work today. I'm fixing her a dinner here at home. The table is already set with crystal, gold and candles. We'll have a salad, chicken and vegetables with tea. Her card is on her plate. I'll have a rose on the plate too. When she walks in the front door, I'll hand her a rose. A second cup of tea in the living room…and I'll hand her a rose. I'll draw her bath with another rose and at bedtime another on her pillow. This is the kind of romance that I believe so many women would like. (Actually, I'd like it too.) But I don't think Yohan has ever appreciated it. I would love for the evening to end in an intimate way, but I know it won't. She'll be home in about 2 hours. I think I'll put this diary aside for now…going to sit and cry a little.

December 11, 2004 (Saturday)

Yohan was out of the house very early. I left by 9:00 am to get a haircut and make copies of our caroling program. I returned home by 10:00 am. Yohan had gone to the Broadway Market to get cheese for pierogis. Over the last several years we had made that trip together. She knows that I always enjoyed that excursion, yet she went without me. I asked her why she didn't ask me to join her—no answer. Then I said never mind, I guess that's something that I shouldn't ask. Once again, my feelings are hurt. She dragged out more Christmas stuff. (I thought she was done.) I really just wish it was January. She's still decorating…she doesn't want me to help…I went and lay on the bed for about two hours. Tonight, we have a rec. council party to go to. We had a nice time. Once home and in bed, I tried to snuggle a bit. But once again she put the brakes on it right away.

"Not tonight, you kept me up last night."

The previous night, we spent an hour or so talking about her birthday. My perception is that she did not enjoy everything that I had planned for her. She actually had offered no expression at all, facial or verbal. I should be used to it...but when our daughter gave her a gift, she gushed all over it. Can't I get just a tiny bit of 'gush?' I showed her my journal. I'm not sure if she knew I had been writing one. She has silently expressed her lack of love for me many, many times. She hurts my feelings every day. I want to help her. I want to do the right things to help us, but at the same time I'm so depressed that I've lost all confidence in myself. I'm afraid to do anything around the house, because she might not want me to do 'things.'

December 12, 2004 (Sunday)

In the evening, Yohan went to her parent's house to pick up her birthday gift. This coming Christmas would have been my 34th with her family and the 'break bread Polish tradition.' Their tradition has become mine...but I'm not allowed to participate any longer. How could they do this. They took my family from me on Thanksgiving and now Christmas is around the corner. They are hateful, hurtful people. I'll never forgive them.

December 14, 2004 (Tuesday)

I don't know what to do; I just don't know what to do. It's clearly evident that she has absolutely no love for me. I don't think there's any left in her heart. Should I pursue what I want? How can I when she has offered nothing emotional to me. Just one sincere kiss would do it. Too many things are wrong, and nothing is right. I can't even organize a few boxes in the basement. She says I lost one? I did not throw away anything. I need someone to love me as a man. I need to be able to walk past Yohan and have her WANT me. I need her to touch me because she wants to, not because she feels some obligation. I need to be desired as a GOOD husband, father and a man, a soon to be 51-year-old man with everything in good working condition. Overall, I look okay, feel good, and dress well. I need to be loved…been living in limbo far too long.

Our son has his own house; our daughter is working 3-11 shifts. These are times I've dreamed of. Yohan and I alone, a kiss in the kitchen—sex on a chair—on the floor—on the table. Instead, I've been crying and can't stop. This should be the best time of our lives, and I feel like I'm dying. We have not had sex since soon after her accident at work. What am I going to do? I don't think my rope is much longer.

December 15, 2004 (Wednesday)

Yesterday evening, I really thought for a long time. After all of this time, I finally realized why she has never 'cut me loose'—why has she kept me on a string all of this time. She needs my paycheck. If we separated and sold the house, we'd each walk away with a few dollars, but she'd still need financial assistance. I asked her about this and she said, "Yes, that's true, but it's not why she's holding on."

Hypothetically, I asked her if she would mind if I sought a physical relationship outside of our marriage, since she had no desire for me.

She said, "I'll have to think about it."

REALLY! Shouldn't the answer be NO? I've never had a relationship on the outside, and I don't want to. (Remember the prostitute offer?) I'm thinking of telling two of my friends at work about what I'm going through. I can still put on a good face at work. Yohan went bowling tonight. I had a piece of cake for dinner. *(Okay…that's making me laugh.)*

December 17, 2004 (Friday) My birthday

In the morning, Yohan presented me with a bottle of wine then off to work. After work, we worked in the kitchen baking for a bake sale. We ordered Chinese food and ate in. Her company Christmas party is tomorrow afternoon 1:00 pm till 6:00 pm. She told me she'll be going out early in the morning because she was being treated to breakfast. I didn't ask who's treating (it must be her friend DAVID…*oh won't that be nice*). I know who's treating. This ruined my day. It's my birthday, and she announces her date with another.

December 18, 2004 (Saturday)

The Christmas party wasn't bad. Yohan seemed proud to introduce me to her co-workers. However, when she introduced me to Glenn, he made a comment about all of the flowers that I send her. (I don't even know the company address.) Later, she told me that David sent her flowers on her birthday. (But Glenn's comment was 'all the flowers…guess she receives flowers often…I thought once a long time ago and many moons away that she told me that David is married…but who knows).

December 19, 2004 (Sunday)

So today we're supposed to make the pierogis. Yeah, I'm into that. Help to make the Christmas Eve dinner that I'm not allowed to attend. The tree has been in the living room for a week now with no decorations on it. I put lights on it one evening and that's where it's at. I wish it was January. I don't think I want to be home when Yohan leaves for dinner on Christmas Eve. Maybe I'll call the BH to see if I can visit at that time. I've been having bad dreams about my in-laws.

I told Yohan that she has managed to exclude me from most of her routines, but I think we need to reserve some 'us' time. And we spoke about 'David' a little. I asked her to break off her friendship with him as the relationship is not conducive to the recovery of our marriage. It's him who she had referred to when she mentioned, "Some of my friends are wondering why I didn't leave you long ago." If she truly wants to get back with me, he can't be in the picture. Also, I want Sundays back. She'll need to visit them on her time, not our time. I hate the Sunday church parking lot questions every week. Her parents and David are no win cahoots. I can smell it. I've seen this step-mother in action many times before. She has intentionally interfered in the marriages of both of Yohan's brothers. She's happy when she creates disruptions, and she feeds on gossip. Yohan and I have both seen her 'pump' children for dirt on their parents…we've spoken about it many times in the past, and can only assume that over the years she has 'pumped' our kids too. If Yohan doesn't agree with these suggestions, then I think I'll ask her to ask her parents if she can stay with them for a while. She says she understands, but is not sure about the visit with her parents, but she'll think about it. If she refuses, I think I just might look into filing for a separation in January. It's not what I want; I just can't be left on a string forever.

December 22, 2004 (Wednesday)

Co-workers took me out for lunch today for my birthday. Yohan and I were not supposed to exchange Christmas gifts, but I know she bought me something. So, I bought her a 'Day of Beauty' today. Hope she likes it.

December 23, 2004 (Thursday)

For the first time, I told two of my co-workers about my current home situation and my Christmas Eve plans. I think they were totally speechless. Supposed to go Christmas caroling tonight in Fells Point with my son and a friend. I was able to get a bottle of 'Polish beer,' and I ask my son to give it to my father-in-law.

December 24, 2004 (Christmas Eve)

Yohan is off today, but I'll be at work. Got off about 90 minutes early so I'm came home. Originally, I was going to go directly to the BH, but it seemed too early. Yohan had a snack tray and two glasses of wine prepared. Kinda nice! Then I went to the BH for about two hours. They had a gift for me. I was touched. (But I had some gifts for them too.)

When I returned back home, I was on my own for about 90 minutes when my family arrived back home. Apparently, no one missed me at the in-laws…Even my favorite Aunt didn't question my whereabouts. Maybe I'm getting used to things, I wasn't in too bad of shape…given everything that has happened. I was almost relieved that I didn't have to be there. My son was aggravated; they sent him to the store across the street to get a bottle of wine. A few minutes later when he returned, they had already completed the Polish tradition of 'breaking bread.' He said that after dinner, he basically sat alone in the living room (out of main activities). Our family was going to *midnight mass* this evening, then opening gifts afterwards. I was pleased that my kids followed my wishes and donated funds in my name to Red Cross, SPCA, OLH-Angels, and Fireman's Boot. I think this is a good thing.

December 25, 2004 (Christmas Day)

Slept till about 10:00 am…didn't quite feel right Yohan fixed a nice breakfast and before I knew it, I was in the bathroom both ends. Was deathly sick all day and well into the evening. Went back to bed and didn't get up till next morning. I was unable to go to my parents' and couldn't even lift my head. Yohan went alone and met our son there. Our daughter had to work.

December 31, 2004 (New Year's Eve)

We had plans to go out for dinner and then a show. It's Friday, and I left work a little early. Yohan was cooking; we're having neighbors over tomorrow. We got dressed and our first stop was at the BH. Just a brief visit to say Happy New Year. I showed Yohan my 'old room.' From there, on to the restaurant. Friends were there and they sent the waitress over to offer a drink. That was nice! After dinner, we went downtown to the theatre (Jesus Christ Superstar). The show was excellent. It was such a nice evening…I had often told Yohan that when the kids were older, I'd like to subscribe to shows and concerts…to have a really good excuse to go out about once a month for dinner and entertainment. This afternoon/evening seemed perfect. Therefore, the dinner and show could have been any evening of the year. But now, once at home again it was suddenly New Year's Eve again. So, I couldn't handle it because of the thought of people exchanging kisses and the perception that everyone is happy and celebrating…everyone except me. I just couldn't handle it, despite the perfect evening. I got undressed and went to bed. This is the time when you're supposed to be with the one you love, kiss passionately and say I love you. We can't do any of that because of Yohan. So, I can't handle New Year's Eve. When she came up to bed, I really did not want her to know that I was crying. TOO LATE…we talked a little and cried through midnight. I told her that I'd been thinking of a separation because I hurt everyday…and just have to do something. She said that she had thoughts of getting close tonight—a little romantic tonight but figured that since I went straight to bed—I was tired. I'd give anything for a sincere night of passion with her but I don't think it's ever going to really happen. During the day, while I was at work, she took our daughter's car to have a flat tire fixed. I knew it, but didn't want to ask where she took the car. *(I knew it had to be David…I don't think I've mentioned this in any of my entries, David is a grease monkey…he fixes cars and works on motors etc.…I try to never judge other people's exterior and I feel really guilty about saying this, but I can't imagine Yohan being with him…he is not at all an attractive person).)* Well…it was just last week when I asked her to break her friendship with him. So much for that. She could have taken the car to the garage right at the end of our street. We're friends with those owners.

I apologized to Yohan for asking her to break that friendship. I know I can't really ask her to do something like that. Tossed and turned all night, didn't sleep well, cried often. Happy New Year.

January 1, 2005 (New Year's Day)

Straightened up around the house, neighbors are coming over tonight. Yohan fixed all of the food, and didn't want anyone to bring anything. The first guests arrived by 6:00 pm and everyone was back home by 11:30 pm. It was a nice evening

January 9, 2005 (Sunday)

We were supposed to go to my cousin's house today for an after-Christmas party. But after church…on the parking lot, Yohan did it to me again. She left me and our daughter, standing on the parking lot while she announced that she was visiting her parents.

I said, "I didn't think you were going to do that on a Sunday morning anymore." I thought she'd agreed that she would visit them on HER time, not on OUR time. She suggested that I go visit my parents. Our daughter chose to come with me. But instead, I decided to just go home. So, she hurt me again…again! So now, I really don't want to visit anyone today. When my daughter and I got home, I decided to call Yohan. So, I called the in-law's house number. Father-in-law answered. I said, "Hi, how are you doing? This is Joe."

He said, "Joe who?" Now he knew who it was, they have caller ID as well as an audio that announces the caller.

I said, "Joe, your son-in-law."

He said, "I don't have a son-in-law." And he hung up the phone. This happened twice. A few minutes later, my daughter used her phone to make the call. For this call, Yohan answered. She said that she was unaware of what had just happened. (But she'll never call her father down for doing it…or even question him.). I told Yohan that she's hurt me again, and I really don't want to go to my cousin's now. I invited her to stay at her parents as long as she'd like, she could stay all day and even eat dinner. There's no reason for her to rush home to me. I advised her to ask her parents if she could move in with them for a while. I'm afraid to leave the house again. I'm afraid that I'm on the edge of self-destruction—in many ways.

She got home a little while later. She doesn't understand. She just does not understand. She's hurting me more than I can bear. She did not ask her parents about moving in. She said that this is her house too and she's not leaving. She's not moving an inch. I'm really thinking about a separation. We talked a lot during the day.

January 10, 2005 (Monday)

After a brief doctor's appointment, I arrived at work a little late. Later, I called Routroville—a Catholic organization that focuses on broken marriages. I should be receiving information in the mail. After that I called a lawyer to ask general information for filing a separation. Before Yohan got home from work, I sat and wrote letters resigning from everything again. I'm just at the end and totally lost. (I can't even go to church anymore…don't want to see anyone. I sent a different letter to our church deacon, asking him to take me off of the Eucharistic Minister list. I just can't go to church right now… (It's the parking lot thing as well as I just don't want to see anyone). Five letters went out in the mail. As difficult as that is…it does lift a bit of weight from me.

To all organizations that I am part of:

Dear Friends,

As I'm sure you recall, it was approximately 26 months ago that I suffered a nervous & emotional breakdown. Circumstances in my life dealt me a hand that I just couldn't bear. At that time, I sunk into a depression that I've still never fully recovered from. As is generally known, when someone is in a depression, the holidays can be devastating. However, I was able to put on a happy face and get through it all. I thought I'd be okay. But...what I didn't know was that just around the corner from the holidays, I would have to endure another life changing realization.

I feel so bad about what appears to be constant flip-flopping. Our organizations deserve someone who is dedicated and willing to make a positive change. Once again, I am not that person...I can't be. I'm hoping that I can make it to work every day. The last time this happened to me, my boss allowed me to sit at my desk and do absolutely nothing for six weeks...I don't think I'll be able to get away with that again.

I consider everyone as good and loyal friends. You've each done a lot for me over these last few years and enabled me to grow. I'll always appreciate your understanding and again offer my sincere apologies...but right now, my life is almost too hard to bear and I just can't take on any responsibilities.

My most sincere regards.

When Yohan got home, I told her all of this. She did not want me to send out letters again...but I have to. Too much is wrong and there's too much pressure. Right now, I can't handle any personal problems, and I can't have anything on my calendar. I must have a clear calendar. It will be hard for me to tell my parents that I won't be in church anymore...We've been meeting them and sitting with them for several years. I mentioned this to Yohan...because I'll have to tell my parents why...would that be okay with her. She said yes, it's okay.

I called my mother. I spoke a lot about my issues. I think I owed that to her. We talked for about 30 minutes or more. She really seems very understanding. I felt good when I hung up.

January 11, 2005 (Tuesday)

Yohan wanted to go to our Tuesday evening dancing. I didn't want to go. Now there's a switch. At work, I found out that I may need to go to New York in about two weeks. I hope not…this kinda upset me. I got slightly emotional and told my manager that I just resigned from all of my organizations—again.

January 14, 2005 (Friday)

A co-worker and I ate lunch out today…then drank lunch. She was able to get me to talk about some of what I've been going through. She insisted that I am her only real friend and she hates to see me hurting like this. At one point I actually began to fill up and started to cry in the restaurant. There's got to be an end to this. At home, I told Yohan about lunch…and drinking lunch (for three hours). She could tell I had a really bad day. She insisted on going out for a dinner, and she'd treat me to 'her driving us.' She probably HAD to. She tried to be a little more caring and affectionate. I ate it up.

January 15, 2005 (Saturday)

After doing the laundry, I spent the afternoon on the couch. I went through some sale booklets and magazines. Feeling down and quiet. I began to go through the book that

Ms. Goldberg (BH) had given me at Christmas. I found that she wrote a note on the inside cover. It really touched me…and I actually had a 'happy cry.'

Hi Joe, if everyone was just like you, what a wonderful world this would be. We miss you! Very, Very Merry Christmas 2004. Love, Ms. Goldberg & grandson.

I'm so glad that I made a positive impact on their lives. That note made me feel better. I think I was meant to find it now.

January 17, 2005 (Monday)

Today is my parents' 52nd anniversary. It's also the anniversary of our first miscarriage—27 years ago. This was on my mind all day. When Yohan got home in the evening, after we had dinner, she was having a cup of tea. I asked her if she knew what today was. I think she was a bit surprised that I was thinking along those lines. Strange, but I still feel as though there's an essence of that first and second child in the house. Their voices and presence never heard never seen but ever present.

January 26, 2005 (Wednesday)

Finally received a return call from Retroville (Catholic service for troubled marriages). They're sending packets of information. It looks like this service will cost about $600.00. Not sure what to think. Hope Yohan will still agree to go. I found out on Sunday that David was at the in-laws for Thanksgiving as well as Christmas Eve. Why is this information always kept from me? I wouldn't be suspicious if I was kept in the loop. I don't like it when 'David information' comes my way, but at least I know it. Oh yeah, I found Yohan's front car seat repaired! David picked her up then dropped her back at work during their lunch break. She didn't even mention the re-upholstery. I've been asking her to get it done for three years. All David has to do is offer to pick her up and it's a done deal. (Kiss kiss…or was his wife there too?)

February 6, 2005 (Sunday)

In some respects, I guess, I've been more accepting of our situation, all I know is I'm not writing in this journal as often as I had. I got a promotion this week at work (AVP). I was completely surprised. The announcement was made on Wednesday. I spent a good portion of my workday responding to congratulatory e-mails. At first, I didn't want to acknowledge it, but eventually did tell my friends on my floor at work and I did call Yohan and tell her. Larry *(Former tenant at the BH)* showed up at my door this week. I wondered how he knew where I lived. He said he just walked the neighborhood till he saw my car. We celebrated my parents' belated 52nd anniversary this past week. The family went out to Sunset for dinner.

February 16, 2005 (Wednesday)

On Friday evening Yohan & I participated in a Retroville weekend. We left right after work and arrived at a Best Western in Burtonsville. We checked in at 7:30 and soon thereafter began the first of 48 hours of presentations and activities. The weekend ended on Sunday evening around 6:00 PM. The food was excellent and hopefully we now have the beginning s of a structured plan on rebuilding our marriage.

My sister called. Mom is in the hospital. Her legs are in bad shape and she's having trouble breathing. She's holding so much fluid, I'm really worried. I called Yohan at work and told her. After work I went to the hospital to visit her. I saw the aid bandage her legs. I was horrified. I'd seen her legs before and they have looked bad…but I was just horrified. Her body seemed very large and fluids were leaking from her legs. After my visit—on my drive home—I began to cry. She seemed so helpless. I tried to comfort her, but I don't know if I really did. I was crying uncontrollably and wondered how much longer her life would be. By the time I was nearing home I was actually hysterical. I just couldn't wait to go in and get a much-needed hug from Yohan. I pulled in front of the house and her car was not there. I fell apart. I lay on the front seat of my car and cried uncontrollably for about 15 minutes before I could regain some composure. I came inside—dropped my coat on the floor, stepped over the mail and went into the bathroom. I thought I had to go. I filled the toilet with blood and tissues. This was the fourth time this week. Still crying, I said, "Why is everything wrong dear God, why can't something be right?" Referring to our marriage, mom, depression, Yohan, blood, in-laws…everything. I finished in the bathroom, came out and sat in the staircase. I noticed the mail that I had stepped over. Our daughter had arranged it on the floor with two Valentines cards. One for dad, one for mom. I opened my card and read the verse. The sad crying immediately turned to tears of elation. I had just cried that everything was wrong. This was the one thing that is right. My daughter will never fully understand the impact that the card had on me.

My mother never came home again. The next four months would be spent in hospital environments. She died on June 20th. She was transferred back and forth from hospital to nursing home (for rehabilitation)... She spent time in several hospitals and Nursing homes. I visited her every day after work...and my father and I would go down to the cafeteria and grab something to eat. Her last three days are detailed in my June writings.

February 20, 2005 (Sunday)

It's 9:00 am as I write this. Yohan's been gone for 60-90 minutes already. I probably won't see her till 1:00 pm or 2:00 pm. Who knows? She had asked me if I was planning on going to the hospital today. I said, "Yes, for a short time. And I was hoping that you would go with me." She made no comment. A few minutes later she left. She leaves early on a Saturday morning, and then I don't see her for 6 or 7 hours. *(Oh my...I wonder where she is.)* On Wednesday, she bowls and doesn't get home until about 9:00 pm. On Monday and Thursday, she goes to Curves and gets home sometime after 7:00 pm. I think she's living the 'married-singles life' that was talked about at Retrouville. She has asked that I introduce her as 'her given name...not a shortened version' from now on. (Split personality? Who knows?)

February 26, 2005 (Saturday)

Yohan and I are supposed to go to a follow-up of Retroville this evening. I've done a lot of thinking this week and I'm drawing some conclusions. When I think of her problems and how far back they go…it's a wonder. A re-thinking of her background:

- Yohan's mom died when she was in second grade. She doesn't remember a whole lot about her, but the memories that she does have are good ones.
- Within 1 year her dad married a woman 15 years younger than he was. The step-mother entered a household that included three children.
- The step-mother wasn't really prepared for what lay ahead. Her life quickly became difficult. She became a tyrant. Before long, Yohan was washing clothes before the school day and hanging them out to dry. She also cleaned the bathroom every morning. After school she'd bring in dry clothes, fold them and iron some of them. She'd then fix or at least start dinner. Weekends were house cleaning—every weekend.
- When I met Yohan, we were 16. I distinctly remember her younger brother washing all of the windows regularly as well as washing and buffing the kitchen floor. Her older brother left the house at either 17 or 18 years old. They didn't know where he went, but come to find out he went to live with his grandparents.

- She wasn't allowed to have friends over and she couldn't belong to clubs like girl scouts. When I would come over, we couldn't stay at her house, and I was not allowed out of the kitchen while I waited for her.
- Yohan and her brothers could never do anything right. Step-mother often had them re-do their work.
- When the new sister was born, Yohan was in charge of most of her care (diapers, bath, put to bed). As the sister got older, Yohan was in charge of doing homework with her. When we were dating, she often would talk about the overwhelming amount of work and responsibilities that she had. She always said that she never did anything right to please her step-mother. And of course, they didn't approve of me as well. So, I was just something else that she didn't do right. Maybe she did just marry me to get out of that house.
- When we announced our first pregnancy, about three years into our marriage, her father said, "Well, if that's what you want." (I can still hear those words). That's all that he said…and the step-mother said nothing. I saw Yohan's disappointment at their reaction, This was just one more thing that she did wrong. With my family, there were hugs and shrieks of joy.
- I believe that Yohan entered our marriage with a very low self-esteem. It was already in place. But I didn't know it. We were young. I always saw in her, an unwavering need to gain a much-needed approval from her father, but she never got it.

February 27, 2005 Sunday

Retroville says that love is not a feeling, it's a decision. I don't really agree with that completely, but I asked Yohan her thoughts. I acknowledged that she doesn't love me, but I asked her about her feelings about me. She said she doesn't know how she feels. I asked her to rate her feelings for me on a scale of 1 to 10. She said she doesn't know which number it would be but it would be a 'pretty low number.' I said that she would need to make a conscious decision to at least like me more or our sessions just won't have much meaning.

March Whatever—Easter Sunday

It's just about noon as I write this today. I've taken a shower, ironed some clothes, and am sitting in my robe having a fresh cup of coffee. Already, I've put some clothes away from yesterday. I'm on my second load of laundry this morning. Ran the dishwasher and then put all of that away. I've fixed eggs, bacon and toast this morning and I've straightened through the house. Yohan left early this morning to meet her step mother at 8:00 am church. Then she and my daughter will join at the in-laws for a traditional Polish breakfast. Her father always says a 'toast.' He and I would have a shot glass of whiskey. The toast is always the same.

"We're thankful that everyone could be here and I hope we're all here next year."

His last few years have seen some health issues. He usually 'fills up' a bit during that 'toast.' I've often thought that he is referring to the possibility of HIM not being here the next year. Of course, this year it's ME not being there.

It's pretty chilly outside today; rain is expected in the afternoon. We're supposed to meet my sister's family at the nursing home to visit mom, then hopefully we can get dad to join us for an Easter dinner at a restaurant about two blocks from the nursing home.

Yesterday, Yohan was out of the house by 7:00 am and returned home about noon. She didn't indicate where she went for five hours. At that early of an hour, I had a feeling that she was meeting someone for breakfast. I wondered if she went to the graveyard (her mother's grave) as well. Yohan goes every year and I think she prefers to go by herself. One time I did go with her…she filled up a little and told me, "I think my mother would have really liked you, Joe." Those exact words—they meant a lot to me then, and they still do.

April 1, 2005 (Friday)

The anniversary of our second miscarriage. This second child was lost about five months into Yohan's pregnancy. We saw the baby—a boy—completely formed. Our boy.

April 19, 2005 (Tuesday) Our 30th Wedding Anniversary

Actually, I did not write a journal entry on this day…but for this book it's important to indicate that it's our 30th anniversary. Over these last several days, I've been writing a poem for Yohan I bought six anniversary cards for her and wrote a poem with six verses. For six days I placed a *card where she'd find it, ending on the 19th. I included one verse in each of the cards.*

On that day in April, When God joined our lives…
So long ago, I gazed into your eyes…
Your gown hand sewn and pearls from your mom…
With starry eyes, we'd 'just begun'
I loved you 'Yohan,' as we kissed goodnight…

On our 5th anniversary, our son you carried…
Our family begins, so pleased we're married…
My radiant wife, I felt such pride…
So proud to be with you, my beautiful bride…
I loved you my 'Hoff,' as we'd greet with embrace…
On our 10th anniversary, you carried our daughter…
Our love is our strength, as our family grows larger…
Realization of dreams, now in our grasp…
Perfect family, perfect marriage, I pray Lord can this last…
I loved you my dear, as we caressed in the morning…

A decade later, sees 20 years…
I understand now, you've hidden some tears…
Wish I could make the hurt go away…
I'd give anything to re-live those days…
I loved you 'Momma,' as we walked hand in hand…

A mid-point in marriage, as we celebrate silver…
Evaluate the past, and plan for our future…
Life for me seems so very kind…
But you're hiding despair, and I've been blind…

And I loved you my dear, as we smiled at each other…

Maturity beckons, as thirty years close…
Good days long gone, what I'd give for those…
Thoughts so clear, in earlier days…
Depression and sadness, has stolen our fire…
I'll love you forever, as we kiss good bye…

Yohan gave me a bottle of wine and a card that was intended for someone who just was 'separated.' She said that is NOT how she read the verse…Who knows maybe it could be read both ways. I gave her two roses. A red one for love and a yellow one for sorrow.

May 4, 2005 (Wednesday)

Wow, it's been a while since I took a few minutes to write. A lot has happened.

Mom had her leg amputated just below the knee. It's been tough on everyone, but mom seems to be okay with it. My friend Larry thinks he had a stroke last week. They tried to reach his ex-wife (no luck). A message was left for me. He refused to get in an ambulance, and refused to go to a hospital. He says if I pick him up, he'll go. So I picked him up and took him to Veteran's Hospital. He was there for five days. When he was released, I brought him back home to the 'shed' he was living in. There's a big celebration coming up in Yohan's family. Her nieces (triplets) will be making their first Holy Communion. There will be about 60 people invited but not me. Her father apparently said that if I show up, he'll leave. He said that he never liked me and that I always acted as though I'm better than him. And he doesn't like the way I never let Yohan finish a sentence. I really don't know where he's coming from. I was hurt and I lashed out at Yohan. But it's not her fault…I apologized to her later. At one point I said that I have his death to look forward to. (Whew…that was hard to write). Now that I've had time to digest the whole 'in-law thing'…I think I've realized that I need to put the whole thing behind me and not worry if I'll ever be invited there again. I think I've already begun to just let it go. Besides, I've been invited to a neighbor's house for a 'drink fest.' We'll see what happens.

I had somewhat of a realization on Monday (the evening before Mom was to have her leg amputated). Weeks ago, when mom was near death (so we thought) I prayed to God to please help me to help the family during these crises. Help me to say the right words and to do what's right for mom & dad and everyone else. Help me to be the strength for all. Steve, my brother, complimented me on Monday evening. We talked on the phone for about 20 minutes. He thanked me for all I'm doing and told me how much dad appreciates it. I was thinking about everything going on…I realized that there were times where even I was unsure of how I was able to put the words together to say what needed to be said and to balance it with compassion and understanding for mom & dad. Also, how was it possible for me to make so many requests to so many medical professionals and get so many quick responses? I cried for a long time in thanks when I realized that my prayers had been answered. I may not be in church lately, but certainly not for lack of belief in God. I'm trying to be a good person, I always thought I was. I want to do Gods work in a way others will see it and be influenced by it. I'm trying to mentor Larry & Paul *(my friends from the BH)* too. "What so ever you do to the least of my brothers…That you do unto me."

May 8, 2005 (Mother's Day)

Yohan was up before me, dressed, but didn't go to church (shocked me). She already ate a small breakfast. I had no plans for today—I also had no gift or card. It just seemed like I shouldn't. She went to her moms and gave her a gift, and then later we visited my mom at the hospital. We gave her 'scratch-offs'…She loved it.

May 9, 2005 (Monday)

I called Gladys today *(good friend who received one of my resignation letters)*, first time I'd talked to her since the holidays. She cried. I explained that I was never mad at her for anything. I just needed a clear calendar. She understands.

June 25, 2005 (Saturday)

Mom passed away on June 20th. My journal entries are regular, but they are not daily. This entry was posted on Saturday, June 25th.

I'm proud to include this particular entry. It's a long one that describes my mother's last three days and how I and our family dealt with her imminent death.

Over the past few weeks, she did amazingly well—even managing to get out of bed and into her wheelchair on her own. But almost overnight she changed. She was extremely tired…sleeping 90% of the time. I questioned her about her medications and then questioned the staff and her doctors. I thought maybe she was overmedicated. This went on for about 10 days. One morning, she was having difficulty breathing, high heart rate and low blood pressure. She was transferred from the rehab facility to the hospital.

My sister Cindy left a message for me at work. I was teaching a class, but went to the hospital immediately thereafter. When I stepped off of the elevator, Cindy and dad were in the hallway (as if they were waiting for me). They had been told that her condition was extremely serious and they'd even spoken about life support options. They had asked her doctor if he would repeat everything to me once I arrived. The staff paged Dr. Manassas, who arrived in the area within a few minutes.

She has a wound on the side of her hip that had apparently turned septic. The poison that was in her body was causing her to sleep. Given her many health issues, there are really no viable options. The doctor had already given mom this news earlier in the afternoon and she indicated that she did not want to be kept alive. Dad had to sign something indicating that he was present when she said that. The doctor wanted our thoughts. I reminded dad and my sister that she asked us a while back to promise to never allow a ventilator to be administered again…they recalled. We all agreed that it appears it may be time to let mom go.

Within the hour, her IVs were pulled, her medications were stopped, and her forced oxygen was changed to just an oxygen tube. With all of this discussion and with all of the activity around her in the CCU, I really had not seen her yet this afternoon. The doctor says that she could last for hours or days…but it wouldn't be weeks. We called my brother Steve and my other sister, Diane. They're both on their way. In the hallway, we discussed Last Rites. I called Father Jack. He's on his way.

We're told now that we can see her (we're expecting her to be asleep). To our surprise, her eyes were wide open. She panicked a little as we walked in.

"What's going on? What's the matter?" She asked. I calmed her down. I don't know where my words came from, but I did calm her down. We all talked just a little…not really saying a whole lot. The nurse said she had been given a stimulant and it would wear off in about 30 minutes. I called dad aside and reminded him that Father Jack would be arriving soon…should we tell mom? We did. I went to her side and assured her that we all know what is happening. Her condition is not good, and that we have asked Father Jack to come and say prayers.

She said, "Okay."

I went down the hallway and sat in a stray wheelchair…Full Emotions. The elevator opened and Father Jack stepped out. I got up, hugged him and cried. I told him that she is aware that he's coming and we went to her room.

By now additional family members had also arrived including my wife. Altogether, there were 10 people in her room.

"Hi there, Mrs. Taylor It's Father Jack from church."

"I know who you are," she replied. From there all present participated in her service. Even mom was able to say the prayers. It was the saddest, happiest, most emotional, most glorious, most beautiful moment of my life. Mom drifted off to sleep & we didn't hear her voice again. A short time later my brother's ex-wife arrived. It was really good to see her. Many hugs, many tears. I was touched later when her son thanked me for greeting his mom so nicely.

Many moments that night I'll have forever. As the hours grew later, Cindy said she's spending the night with mom. We're also still waiting for Diane to arrive from out of town. Some of the family has gone home; some of us opted to stay around till Diane arrived. They arrived at about 2:30 am (delayed due to traffic tie-ups). By 3:00 am, we all left the hospital except Diane & Cindy. Dad was up at 4:00 am the previous morning, so he's working on 24 hours. We're all drained.

Next morning, about 11:00 am, I arrive at her room in the CCU. I find her room empty and the bed being re-dressed. A panic set in…then a nurse tells me she's been moved to another room. I find dad and Diane, we're together again. Mom's asleep and we don't really expect her to wake again. We spend a lot of time talking, crying, laughing and remembering…

Mom opens her eyes; we speak with her but don't want to pressure her to answer. In a voice that sounds of that from an impaired person, she called for dad.

Dad says, "I'm right here."

Then she says, "I love you."

Dad returns the phrase. We all cry. I lean toward her ear and say, "Mom, it's Joe."

Since I was leaning toward her ear, I didn't see her reaction. Cindy said, "Joe look, she wants to give you a kiss."

I turned my head to see her head turned and her lips puckered. I kissed her. I asked her if she was feeling any pain…would she like some pain medication. She shook her head "no." A few seconds later she said, "Do you think it would be okay?" (Referring to the pain medication.) I assured her it's okay…

A few minutes later she had the medication. Mom drifted off to sleep for a short time. Then, "OH MY GOD," she said.

"Mom what's the matter? What do you need?"

"There's an ANGEL," she said. Immediately, I had goose bumps. I felt like I wasn't worthy to be standing in the room. Mom's eyes were wide opened and focused at an area on the ceiling.

Dad said, "What's the angel doing?"

Twice she replied, "He's just standing there."

I told her to take his hand when he reaches for you. Over the next day or so, she made some noises, but no real audible words. Her words referring to the angel were her last words.

Cindy said that in the last two days, the few words that she's said have been words that made us feel so good, so comfortable…and I agree. Dad's chair is the closest to her face. Throughout this time, he's been so caring, so gentle, and so tender. His words to her summed up a lifetime just by their tone. He brought tears to our eyes as he softly sang tunes from their day. *Let Me Call You Sweetheart* brought tears. He kissed her cheek and rubbed noses. He insisted that she was participating in the nose rubbing. Maybe she was. Cindy and her son spent the night (Sunday night).

I arrived in her room about 3:00 pm. My sisters, little Charlie and Dad were there. Her condition appeared to be the same. Her breaths were shallow and seemed to be so far apart—just like the day before. With each exhale, her vocal cords expressed an involuntary sigh. We wondered aloud if today would be the day or will the Lord let us keep her for a bit longer. Over the next hour we all cried at her bedside, we laughed just a bit, and we wondered what was next. Dad sang a few songs, ever so softly. My heart was full.

At about 4:20 pm, Charlie said, "Look, I think her breathing has changed." The five of us stood around her bed. It had changed. Our eyes filled as we gathered a little closer. Her breaths were so very faint and so far apart. A definite difference. The exhale was so weak. The sigh that we'd been hearing was no longer there. We focused on each other and we focused on mom. Studying her face…watching her breathe.

There were few words exchanged during this time. At 4:30, she drew her last breath.

Dad was the one who said, "I think she's gone."

Diane said, "I think you're right, Dad."

I personally thought they were wrong…I just thought the next breath was taking a little longer. But I was wrong. We all hugged and cried. The feelings were so mixed. Instantly, I was overwhelmed with a sense of loss. At a time when our hearts were so full, there was a sudden profound emptiness. But I also realized what I'd just witnessed. Her death was beautiful. It was as beautiful and fulfilling as life itself. In an instant, her entire life had more meaning than it ever had before. Her childhood growing up in a dysfunctional family, her mother a prostitute, her father out of her life, her brother a child molester and sexual offender, her 52 years of marriage, her family, her joy, her depression, her 10 years in a wheelchair and her last four months away from her home. All of this had a reason and a purpose that is now multiplied 100-fold.

Once again, I felt somewhat unworthy for my presence to be allowed as THE LORD was doing His work. But…I'm there for a reason. Thank you, Lord, for allowing me to realize that death is life. Mom's death passes on a torch of responsibility to all of us that were close to her. And to all who experienced emotions with her. I am validated, and now have a whole new purpose. A purpose that I've just begun to embark on. I don't know what God has in store for me, but I'm going to do it to the fullest.

In the last hour of her life, I whispered in her ear, "Mom, when you get there, tug on His sleeve and ask for his special blessing for Yohan and me…thank you and I love you." Now I'm feeling a bit guilty asking for my needs in the face of God's work. But I hope we get the guidance that we need. We all made calls to our immediate family members.

I'm not sure how any of us could propose how we might choose to die, but given all the pain and agony that mom had endured—then leading up to the serenity of her final minutes—I would not opt to change even one second of that time. As I think on her death, I hear a beautiful poem. In and of itself, she realized an art form. An art form as yet undefined. But an art form that endures forever and is appreciated for an eternity.

The beauty of one's life culminates in the magnificence of one's death. Thank you, Dear Jesus.

After about 20 minutes, Cindy and I went out of her room to ask a nurse to come in. The attendant that I'd ask was apparently the wrong person…she said you'll have to get Anna. So, I turned to Anna who said, "I'll be with you in a moment—I'm counting work."

So, Cindy and I stood and watched. After about two minutes I interrupted and asked who else could I address, as our mother had just died. With that Anna began to cry and apologized. She had no idea why we needed her. She said that she lost her husband just a few weeks ago. She apologized profusely and had tears running down her face. She asked us to go back into mom's room…she'll be in in a minute to answer our questions.

Cindy and I returned to mom's room…Anna came in and I did all of the talking. We waited to know what was next. With our questions answered we wondered what was next. We all said good bye to mom again and walked down the hall. I will NEVER forget that walk down the hall. We were walking into a new dimension, turning a page and finding a new chapter. I'm nervous about Dad, hope we can offer the support he needs. We met at Dad's house— jokingly, Diane & Cindy voted me to be the new 'boss' of the family. I was authorized to sit in mom's chair and to begin making arrangements and calling additional family.

The Beauty of One's Life

Reflections as our family witnesses our mother's death.
(I wrote this in my journal during the week of Christmas
2005, but find it appropriate to insert it at this point.)

Labored Breaths, as life's a strain.
Unsure of surroundings, enduring much pain.
Love warms the heart, approaching unknown.
The Final Day beckons, from whence it comes.

Shallow Breaths, Far in-between.
The soul relaxes, Life is serene.
Glories from Heaven, as an angel appears.
The moments are precious, the hour is near.

A Single Breath, Becomes the last.
The instant unclear, A whole life has passed.
Our GOD is present, as this servant expires.
This undying quest, the ultimate desire.

Left standing Empty, But full of each other.
How do we cope, With the death of our mother?
A Comfort realized, With that last Breath.

The Beauty of one's Life,

Culminates...

In the Magnificence of one's Death.

August 24, 2005

I simply have not taken the time to write in the journal...but want to just mention a few things about mom's funeral. Everything went really well. Dad insisted on 2 days of viewing...and that's ok. The funeral parlor was mobbed...many guests came to visit. Ultimately Cindy & I wrote out 140 'thank you' acknowledgements. My son works for Baltimore County Police department, and was able to arrange for a police escort from the funeral home to the cemetery (about a 20-mile ride over the beltway). Mom would have absolutely loved it.

So, regarding my in-laws: They sent a mass card, but did not attend and did not call. They live within a five-minute WALK of the funeral home and did not have the decency or courtesy to visit in the wake of my mom's death. Unbelievable! As many times as my parents were invited to events at their house for affairs that required a gift (they only wanted the gifts). My in-laws are the grandparents of my two children. And my children lost a grandparent...and they offered no support or acknowledgement. Truly they are hateful, hurtful, stubborn people. Yohan's sister and husband attended. When I saw her, I went to her and hugged her and said (during the hug), "I'm so glad that you came, I really appreciated this very much." As I drew back from that hug, to see her face, I realized that she would not look at me. She kept looking to her right as if something was drawing her attention. (There wasn't anything.) She never uttered even a single word to me. I have never experienced such rude and ignorant behavior. Never. Without a doubt, one of the most selfish people I've ever known. Certainly, her mother's daughter. I was glad, however to see that some other relatives of Yohan's did attend…I very much appreciated that.

Of course, I wrote thank you cards to them and made a copy of my words, because I was afraid it would be mis-represented. To my in-laws I wrote:

Dear XXX,

Thanks so much for sending a mass card for my mother in the wake of her death. It was a kind gesture and much appreciated by me and by my family. I'm sure that Yohan has kept you updated on her progress or lack thereof in recent months. I was with her when she took her last breath. So sad, so peaceful so beautiful. I began having a re-occurring dream several months ago, where you both came to her funeral. In that dream, with your attendance, everything became okay. (Yohan knows of this dream.) I'm very sorry that you felt unable to attend.

It's one dream that I would have loved to see come true. My apologies for this digression.

Once again, and on behalf of my family,
Our thanks and my sincere regards.

September 11, 2005 (one entry to cover about 3 weeks)

This past week, for the 1st time in years—Yohan touched me, softly, gently, briefly in an intimate way. It's probably been at least a year since she's touched me in that way at all. Any previous times that she may have touched me…I'd ask her to do so. This time she did it on her own. I'm not sure if she wanted to or if she just thought she would 'treat me.' Either way, I'll take it.

She bought a truck last week—she scouted out vehicles on her own—left me out of that loop. I didn't even know she was looking. I really did feel left out. She asked me to go to the dealer with her to see her choices (two choices). When we arrived at the dealer, Yohan's sales representative was familiar to me, and then the woman made a mention of David. Turns out that the only reason we were at this particular dealer was because the sales representative was a friend of David's. It hurt my feelings that once again Yohan chose to not tell me everything. I really wouldn't care, just don't like to find out stuff backhanded. After talking with the sales representative, turned out that she is also a friend of my former landlady at the BH.

Mom's grave plaque came in and was installed at the end of August. I took Dad to see it. I broke down. Once again, I guess her death seemed so final. It's been tough to go through. Dad went to all of the Concerts in the Park with me. My son, daughter, nephew, sister and her husband joined us at many. Of course, Yohan attended none of them. My daughter helped me make a giant 'thank you card' that I had most of the concert attendee's sign. We presented it to Mark (the organizer) to commemorate 15 years of 'Concerts in the Park.' We went to a 'political picnic' recently and met my brother's girlfriend (Helen) as well as her brother who was in town. They are native to Guam…seemed very nice. We took Dad to the State Fair last week. While there we ran into Yohan's half-sister and family on several turns. She spoke with Yohan, but wouldn't look at me. She is one of the most selfish people that I've ever known.

I had two weeks of vacation at the end of August…running into Labor Day. It was during this time last year that I moved into the BH for three-plus months. At that time, I fell apart when I asked Yohan if she thought we were doing any better. Her reply was that she didn't know. I don't dare ask her again this year—why set myself up for disappointment. She doesn't love me and as a result I have no confidence to organize or accomplish anything. I just exist for now. I'm not happy, but for the most part I've stopped crying. If only one time she could say, "I think I'm starting to love you." I'd soar like an eagle. I don't see that happening.

September 21, 2005

Yohan's father came home today after spending a few days in the hospital. Heart issues. They've discussed a cauterization as well as a pacemaker, but opted for medication for now. Yohan visited him a few times. On Sunday, Yohan & I were near the hospital. I offered to go to the hospital and sit in the waiting room while she visited. So we did that…for about an hour. After recently losing my mother and knowing everything that she went thorough, I know her father has got to be scared. I think he's 82. As much as I don't care to see him again, I find that I do still care for him. After 35-plus years, how can I not. I mailed him a get-well card and enclosed a 'scratch-off.' I wrote:

Just a quick note to let you know that I've been thinking about you and hope that you'll soon be feeling better.
Take Care,
Joe
Good Luck with the scratch-off.

After I mailed the card, I told Yohan about it, just in case she gets 'flack' about it.

I gave some of Mom's clothes to my former landlady a few weeks ago. She really appreciated them. Already I've seen her wearing some of Mom's outfits. I'm glad. I'm slowly getting back into things again, but I don't want to organize anything yet.

November 25, 2005 (day after Thanksgiving)

Can't believe it's been two months since I've written anything. A lot has been happening. I'm off from work today, using some vacation time. It's just after 12:00 (noontime). My two kids met at 4:00 am to go shopping (Black Friday). They wanted me to go but I was afraid that the Christmas Spirit would depress me. A week or so ago, Yohan and I were doing some shopping, and a very sad feeling overtook me and we had to come home. Yohan is at work today, but yesterday, she fixed a thanksgiving dinner for Steve, Helen, Dad, our son, Larry & Paul. (Larry & Paul were friends from the boarding house). Larry provided the turkey…as all employees where he was working received one. Our daughter had to work. This seemed like a very unusual mix of people, but everyone had met earlier as a summer 'political picnic.' I had been dreading this holiday, and it was only a few days earlier when Yohan & I made this decision. It was a quiet afternoon, and kinda nice. Yohan and I always did enjoy preparing for quests. She still ate dinner with her family, before coming home to join in our dinner. But I guess it worked out just fine.

Yohan and I had another conversation about divorce. I actually believe her when she says that she is perfectly content…and she'd like to live the rest of her life in her current situation. On the other hand, I'm so sad that at times it's absolutely unbearable. She still can't say I love you. I guess she's being honest with herself. I still can't believe it. It tears me apart and still destroys my drive. She's 'touched' me once or twice. I wondered if it was an accident. We haven't made love in five years. She says that's not accurate. She's also quite content to never make love again. I'm dying for some attention; would it be so hard? I hope I can make it through the next few weeks.

Larry & Paul (friends from the BH) moved into my neighbors' upstairs apartment two weeks ago. Yohan was able to recommend Larry for an entry level job at a place that she had previously worked at. They're paying my neighbor $500.00 a month. Their sister is coming over to prepare a nice dinner for them. Another brother refused to come. That brother does have a job, but lives in his car. How is it that three brothers are all just barely living in the streets? Yohan is putting a box together that she plans on giving to a homeless man that lives in a makeshift tent on Pulaski Hgwy.

December 17, 2005 (Saturday, my birthday)

I'm having my 2nd cup of coffee. Clothes are in the washer and drier, our daughter is still sleeping. Yohan left for her morning routine about an hour ago. It's 8:20 am now, I dropped Larry off at 7:00 am to fulfill a community service obligation. For the last three weeks, Yohan has been dragging out Christmas decorations. She took a vacation day to put lights up our front. Everything looks nice, but I wish it was February. We're supposed to go out later today to get a Christmas tree. She wants to re-arrange furniture to put the tree near the fireplace…but I don't care to do that. We'll see. I've already cried some this morning. Not too sure if I can make it through the day, just don't know.

Dad and I went to Macy's. I wanted to pick up a necklace for Yohan. Actually, we already exchanged gifts last week, when we bought a jewelry chest and a wine rack and agreed that they were our gifts. But I wanted to do this. I wish and I wish and I wish. And I pray and I pray and I pray. And I cry and I cry and I cry.

I still haven't put away the picnic table or covered the porch swing. Maybe I'll do it today, but I just don't feel like it. Before Thanksgiving, Paul helped me take out screens and clean windows on the first floor, but I haven't done the upstairs. Right now, the upstairs is a complete disaster. It's filled with boxes and gift bags…most of which is going to people that I won't see. Last night Yohan was telling me about her step mother's woes surrounding fixing Christmas

Eve dinner and about hiring a Santa Clause. I tried to listen and appear interested, but I really don't care. It hurts me so much that my kids might go there again. I know it's their grandparents (yeah right). I think I'd be okay if they just chose to visit them from time to time, but it hurts me when they accept a 'family' invitation, when the 'entire family' is not included. For them to attend without me sends a statement of support for my ex-laws.

Maybe when all of this is over, I'll approach Yohan again in January or February for the possibility of counselling again. I wish I was dead—then these hurt, confused, sad feelings wouldn't be.

December 26, 2005 (this entry covers December 23rd)

There's so much junk around the house that it looks like a 'Dollar Store,' but I really don't care. We went Christmas Caroling on the 23rd at the Polish Home club. Yohan dropped us (my two kids, me & Matt) off at the location. Larry, Paul and their sister arrived separately, but we stayed together. When caroling was over, Yohan met us back at the hall, but she was reluctant to do so. She never seems to really enjoy herself. My cousin was there too with her son and her boyfriend. The evening ended around 11:30. I loved it.

We were home by midnight. Due to my kids' different work schedules, we agreed to do our gift exchange on THIS evening. Yohan ordered pizza and the four of us sat in the living room. They knew in advance that I was not going to participate in an exchange. Yohan gave me a shirt. I gave her the diamond neckless. She showed no emotion, and didn't even show it to the kids. I thought she might wear in ton Christmas Eve or Christmas Day…but she didn't. *(no 'gushing' for me).*

We made pierogis on the 24th. I had asked Yohan to get extra ingredients, as I promised some for Larry, Paul, Connie & Harry. She says that she bought extra, but the yield appears to be even less. This batch will go to the ex-laws. We may make more later in the week for me. I helped her load up the car and she went to the ex-laws at about 4:30. I think it was after 9:00 when she returned home. I guess she had a good evening. Our son joined her, but our daughter had to work. I stayed home. Larry and Paul came over and we watched Forrest Gump. I gave Larry a case of beer and Paul a gold cross/chain. Yohan had the cross blessed. Paul loved it. He'd talked about wanting one.

On Christmas day, Yohan, our daughter and me met Dad at church. Weeks prior, we offered a $250.00 donation to have Mom's name memorialized at the 'pew' where she sat in her wheelchair. Surprisingly, the plaque was in place…I couldn't make myself look at it. Later we were meeting at Dad's house to spend the day. Yohan was very quiet, she hardly said two words all day. My emotions are in my throat. I'm ready to cry all morning/day, but I'll try to smile and look happy. On the way to Dads, I had tears running down my face. Yohan didn't say a word. I'll never get used to her insensitivity. Our day was okay. My sister and Yohan brought the food. We did not exchange with Dad.

Dana called Yohan. The ex-laws took her father to the hospital. Later in the day, her step-mother called to say he has pneumonia and congestive heart failure. OH, how I long for Christmas past and Christmas future…Just not THIS Christmas.

December 27, 2005

Yohan and I had one of our talks last night. I started it as usual. I'm not sure why I continue to hope, but I do. She offered nothing, and refused to answer.

"What do you want, Yohan?"

At work I took a long walk around the harbor by myself. As I strolled around the edge, I had thoughts of just stepping into the cold dark water with my hands to my sides, and just letting myself sink. I know I won't do that, but the thoughts were there. I've thought again about separating, but that wouldn't fix my broken heart. I couldn't afford an apartment with the house…We'd have to sell the house and each get our own apartment. In my mind, I've picked out one or two pieces of furniture—Yohan can have the rest. I just don't care. I'd pay Yohan's rent as well as mine. I love her very much. She has broken my heart.

January 3, 2006

Her father has been hospitalized since Christmas. She called me at work today, his condition is now 'grave.' She has visited him on most days, she says that a few times he spoke okay, other times he seemed 'out of it.' He keeps pulling out his IVs. It's 7:15 in the evening as I write this. I have no idea how his death may affect our situation. No idea whatsoever.

March 25, 2006

Larry and Paul invited me over for pizza and a few beers…and to watch a movie. I was there for a couple of hours. We spent a lot of time talking and I don't even know what movie was on the TV. At one point Larry yelled at Paul.

"Put that away, we have company."

I glanced over at him to see him masturbating. Paul defended his actions because of the racy movie that we were watching. He also said, "Larry, you know you want to do it too."

They went back and forth a bit over this and I was totally surprised at this entire conversation. Bottom line: before long all three of us were 'doing it.' We were each on separate pieces of furniture and there was no physical contact between us. A few minutes later Paul was using a tissue to clean himself…and a bit later I too needed a tissue. I had never done something like this before. As weird as it was, this was the first time in a very long time, that I was able to share my sexuality in the presence of others. It kinda felt good. *(This was the only time that we ever did this…and we never spoke of it again.)*

May 15, 2006

My ex-father-in-law died on May 15th 2006. I write about it in my July 4th entry. Until now I just haven't written many entries…it often seems redundant to me…same ol' same ol'.

July 4, 2006

It's been a long time (six months). It's 3:40 in the afternoon. I sit alone having a beer. (What a wonderful holiday party!!) I was off from work all of this past week. I volunteered many hours for the 'historical society' as well as for this morning's parade. Its 95 degrees right now. We've really done quite a bit of work around the house these past few months. Just a short time ago I stepped out of our new hot tub. We have new decking as well as an enclosed back porch. Our daughter is at work today, our son & Yohan both left to go to visit the step mother. Apparently, Dana finished making a bench for Yohan…she supplied those materials for the bench two years ago. After they get the bench, she'll bring a bucket of chicken home for dinner. We're planning on going to our church lot to watch fireworks, but I hear thunder in the distance.

My ex-father-in-law died on May 15th (just a few weeks ago). I enjoyed going to the funeral to see all of the relatives and to 'catch-up' a bit. As for Yohan's immediate family, only one person spoke with me and said that it was good to see me. I teased him and suggested that he's probably not allowed to be seen speaking with me. He said he's not part of that 'stuff.' I enjoyed our conversation. On the morning of the funeral, before anything started, I turned around and found myself face to face with the step mother. I stepped forward, embraced her and said that I was sorry to hear about everything they'd been through over these last several months. I mentioned that I know it must have all been a rough road. As I stepped back, I noticed that her arms were at her sides. She never returned a simple embrace, and she wouldn't even look at me. She kept her head turned sideways. She said nothing…nothing. Not even a basic 'thank you.' As I turned away, I noticed that one of her grandchildren witnessed this. Did he see how cold her heart was? I went back to her house after the funeral for a luncheon. At least 40 people attended. I've not spoken to her since that morning. Enough of that, she's out of my life.

September 6, 2006 Labor Day weekend

This weekend closes a two-week vacation for me. Altogether, I'll have 18 days off. It's about 2:00 pm on Saturday. I sit at home alone; it's raining and I'm having a cup of coffee. During my time off I've: Volunteered for the historical society, our community association, cut out shrubbery and trees in my yard, cleaned the 1st floor of our house. Larry & I cleaned out shrubbery in a neighbor's yard, and cleaned the hot tub. Tomorrow, I'll be volunteering all day for Defender's Day. So far, I haven't spent even a single day relaxing and doing nothing. Next week is dumpster day then Yohan & I have invited a few neighbors over for a cookout. I feel as though all of my work done on the outside has been very much appreciated. But my work done in our yard and home…there is no appreciation. Nothing has changed here. Nonetheless, I find my work to be self-satisfying. Yesterday, I worked in the house from about 8:00 am till about 4:30 pm (stopping only for lunch). I even did all of the laundry, and cleaned all of the hardwood floors. When Yohan came in after 5:00 pm, the first thing she did was criticize me for not checking the windows upstairs when it began to rain. After that she reversed a minor change that I made in the kitchen (without saying a word). Later, she complained that I took out the screen from the kitchen sliding door. She says she'll put it back up. Still later, she rejected my thought of eliminating some of the drinking glasses that we have (we have five shelves of glasses), since we don't have enough space for food and staple goods. By 10:00 pm, I realized that she must have gone to bed…and didn't even say good night. I found her sleeping at 10:05 pm. And I wonder why I grow sadder every day.

I just glanced at writings that I entered earlier in this journal…including the 30th anniversary poem. So now I'm crying.

Labor Day 2006

It was a quiet day. By evening (about 7:00), I got in the hot tub, and surprisingly Yohan joined me. We exchanged small talk. I moved closer to her and asked if I could kiss her. We kissed—long, slow, smooth, wonderful. It was the nicest kiss we've had in years. I was that close to telling her how much I love her, but I didn't want to ruin the mood. Paul hopped the fence; said he heard our music playing. When he realized that Yohan & I were alone, he went back home. Within 10 minutes Larry hopped the fence, and motioned for me to come here. I said no…you come here. He was reluctant. He said Paul tried to hurt himself…cutting his wrist several times with a razor.

I said, "I'll be right over, let me put dry clothes on."

I found Paul huddled in a ball in a corner (he has been a psychiatric patient). He had a towel wrapped around his wrist. He was a mess. He was bleeding and crying and said that he really didn't mean to do it. I asked Larry to leave us alone (Larry doesn't handle this kind of thing very well). I spoke with Paul for about 20 minutes until he agreed to let me take him to the hospital. All three of us went. Before the evening was over, I had Paul's blood on my hands and down my arm. I don't really know what happened. I wondered: Did Paul see us, and think that I was happy…then realized how depressed HE was? He had seemed okay, then 10 minutes later he attempted suicide. He spent the night in the hospital…next evening he seemed fine. I guess it's pretty easy for all of us to deceive others regarding our happiness. I wonder how many people think that I've recovered.

September 9, 2006

On the Saturday after Labor Day, we had a cookout, inviting some of our neighbors. Altogether about 25 people attended. Dad came too. The cookout started at 3:00 pm and the last group of neighbors left at about 2:30. Everyone had a nice time.

September 15, 2006

I received an e-mail at work today…one of those where many names were copied or forwarded on to. I don't usually pay much attention to those 'lists', but I spotted a name that I recognized and singled it out. I sent her an e-mail asking if it was her. Surprisingly, later that day, she responded and it was who I was thinking of. She was glad to hear from me. We only exchanged a few lines each after that, but she said if I'd like to talk, she'd like to listen. Of course, I'm not sure about this, but I think if I wanted to, we could become more than just friends. But I couldn't do that to Yohan, and I'd still have a total lack of confidence. It is making me think though…how much longer should I remain in limbo? I've been crying again the last week or two (a lot). Yohan seems happy and no one cares if I am.

September 16, 2006

It's 11:00 am as I write this. I'm home alone. Yohan left after 7:00 am for her routine. I cried a bit this morning, then got up, went to Home Depot…bought some flowers and dressed up the community playground. Hoping that the satisfying feeling will help me feel better. I took a shower and am now on the back porch. I'm thinking about how we used to have sex on the back porch a time or two every summer, either on a lounge chair or the porch swing. I guess it's been five summers since that last happened. This January will be six years since we've had sex. I can't stand it. I'm not a complete person. There's a basic need to share intimacy…just to feel like someone wants me. She has no interest whatsoever. But she used to love it (on the porch) She was always ready. Yes, I have tears in my eyes again. I know I must have a place in heaven with my name on it. My clouded thoughts are a living hell…right here on earth.

September 19, 2006 (Tuesday)

A very somber mood for me today. After work, we had a nice dinner on the back porch. Steak on the grill, corn on the cob, and glass of wine each. I realized though, I was on the quiet side. We exchanged small talk. Later at about 8:00pm, she was on the porch and I walked past to get in the hot tub. She said oh, maybe I'll join you. In a way that would be nice, but in a way I wanted to be alone. We sat in opposite corners for a while, my eyes closed. Eventually she moved to a closer seat. I thought this might be the start of something. I moved closer to her and put my arm around her. She did too. But I'm so overwhelmed—my eyes filled up and I began to speak.

"You think you have a good plan for life, but we're not where I'd hoped we'd be at this stage of our game."

She thought I was referring to financial matters. I said no, our relationship. I began to cry.

I said, "Yohan, I love you so much, so much. I don't know what I'd do if you weren't in my life." She was quiet. I said, "I want to tell you every day that I love you, but I can't. I want to embrace you, kiss you, but I can't. I want to woo you again, but it's hard. I want to touch you tenderly, but I can't. I want to be touched. But all of this is so hard because I know in my heart that you don't really want me to say I love you—you don't want me to be cute with you. You don't really want me to embrace your or touch you. Am I right, Yohan?"

She said YES, she said yes, she said yes. She doesn't want any of the above. Once again, I just fell apart. I'm not really sure why I fell apart though…I already knew all of the above. I could feel it in my heart, that as God sees my soul, I love her with all of my heart. She does not want me for any more than a companion. I'm writing this on Wednesday, and I didn't sleep a wink last night. Yohan cried a little, she put her arm around me. But the few words she offered gave no comfort. I've been crying for several years now. I just don't know what to do. I had almost thought we'd get 'closer' in the hot tub, but instead it only re-enforced our separation. What's happening in my life? I can't stand it. I asked her if she feels happy. She said she feels content. I wish I were dead. Another day in my own darkness.

November 14, 2006 (Tuesday)

Yohan's Aunt Jenny was diagnosed with breast cancer. We went to visit her on Sunday (all four of us). As we visited her, she seemed okay. I managed to get a few chuckles out of her, and Yohan combed her hair out into a style. We stayed for about 90 minutes. As we were leaving my ex-step-mother-in-law came in alone for a visit. Not a whole lot was said.

Our budget is extremely tight right now, after spending a lot on our back-yard space. It seems that when things get tight, I really get the urge to spend…as if to say what's the use? I'd like to be out of debt when I'm 62. I'd like to be a full-time volunteer…However, I paid for dinner today, as well as treated at the checkout line in Ross (for four). Spent a few hundred dollars. Who cares?

Aunt Doris passed away in October. We had visited her at the hospital as well. It was good to catch up with my cousins at her funeral. I was a pall bearer and so was my son. About a month before that, I took Dad to a funeral for one of his cousins (who had been hit by a car). Sickness and funerals as we sail into autumn.

Thanksgiving is in two weeks. Of course, I'm dreading the holidays. Now that I think of it, I cried on the way to work today. I wonder if it's the season? I have a vacation week scheduled for after Thanksgiving. I'm planning on painting the 'big room' at our community hall. I also thought I might do some fall house cleaning. (Some windows/screens etc.) Oh, I don't know if it's worth it. Truly, I live with two slobs. As I write this, I'm in our bedroom. Yohan has clothes (unfolded) piled on the loveseat. A laundry basked is stacked over two feet above the rim with clean clothes. A few clothes are folded and on the floor. There are clothes hanging on the door. Clothes are on the railing and clothes are downstairs on the kitchen table. There's a large box filled with bags in the bedroom too. There's also a box of Avon stuff on the floor too. As I sit here, there are 14 deodorant/powder/perfume/crème containers on Yohan's night table. Her dresser is cluttered with boxes and bags too. Oh, all of the clothes are clean…none of them are mine. On the bathroom sink there are 16 products on the vanity. Dirty clothes are always on the floor (towels too). She refuses to buy a larger hamper or even to get a 2nd hamper for our daughter's room. Our daughter's room smells like dog pee, but I don't think they would agree. Clothes and clutter dominate everything. There are boxes and projects stacked in the sewing room as well as clothes that permanently hang on the door. The library (downstairs) is filled with Avon stuff. Yohan's cabinets almost can't be seen. Boxes and clutter are all over the extra file cabinets. Our daughter has enough schoolwork and other stuff in the living room to fill a large trash bag. Yohan has several bags/baskets in there too. In the foyer, there are 3 pairs of shoes. In the kitchen, we couldn't sit at the table if we wanted to. It's surrounded with dog toys, recycling and Avon boxes stacked up. Did I say I was

thinking about cleaning? None of the 'stuff' is mine, and
I'm not appreciated when I do try to clean things up a bit.
So…NO, I'm not going to do any house cleaning.

December 2006

Just a Simple 'I Love You' (A Song)

We were two young lovers, back in the day,
Fresh out of high school, married in May.
I'd kiss your soft lips; you'd stroke my hair.
I wanted for nothing, as long as you're there.
Just a simple 'I love you' is all that we knew.

Our family's now growing, nothings the same,
But I didn't know it, you'd never complain.
Your eyes lost their sparkle, your lips never smile,
What can't you tell me? Let's talk for a while.
Just a simple 'I love you' is all I desire.

Words finally offered, have broken my heart.
What should I do dear? Where should I start?
I cry every day now; Nights are lonely and dark.
What did I do dear, that put out your spark?
Just a simple 'I love you,' please tell me that phrase.

We're living apart now, and months have gone by.
I don't understand it, I just don't know why.
I dream of your soft lips, and the smile I once knew.
Please let's start over, just me and you.
Just a simple 'I love you' is all that I need.

March 10, 2007

I spent my first night ever in the hospital the other night. After having chest pains for the third day, I was getting scared. I had taken Larry & Paul to the Dollar Tree after work. As I waited in the car, I decided that I have to go to the hospital. After I brought them home, I poked my head in our front door and announced to Yohan that I hadn't felt good for several days, and was going to the emergency room. I told her that I'd be fine and I didn't want her to waste her evening at a hospital. She looked dumbfounded as I walked back outside. As I started to pull away, she opened the front door to say she would take me. I refused. I was just so afraid that she wouldn't care, that I didn't want to give her the chance to not care. As I was driving off, I started to feel guilty, crying, lonely, un-loved, nobody cares. After some tests, I was home the next day with a clean bill of health. Stress. Also last week I was re-assigned at work, and some of my work team was 'let go.' I think this added to my stress feelings.

Thanksgiving 2007

Yesterday, with Yohan's okay, I sent her step-mother an e-mail—requesting that we bury the hatchet. Yohan approved the text before I sent it. I've saved the e-mail and submit it at this time.

Dear (step-mother),

Yohan & I have spoken about the rift between me and your family, and she is aware of my feelings and I have shown her this e-mail before I sent it to you.

Now…I'd like to offer an 'olive branch' to you at this time. I think it's imperative that we try to cast aside some of the negative feelings that we have for one another. I don't know about you, but it's been very hurtful to me. For the 2nd time in as many years I suffered a breakdown as a direct result of this 'rift.' However, it's not ME that concerns me most…It's my family.

There's no question that the rift between us is hurtful to Yohan and our kids. It is with this in mind that I hope you'll consider burying the hatchet…or at least digging a hole for the hatchet. We certainly don't have to hug and embrace, but I'd like to be civil to one another…so that we can be in each other's company and even speak to one another. As God is my witness, I don't understand the rift. And at this point I don't even care to. I just think it's important to close the gap a little and move on.

So, what do you think? Will you accept the olive branch? I hope so.

I've receipted this e-mail, so I'll be able to tell when you opened it. Of course, I'm at work at the time I've sent it…Please feel free to respond back via e-mail, however it may be possible that I'll be leaving early today, and my not get any response that you may decide on. If that's the case, please respond to Suzanne.

I don't want this e-mail to be some sort of 'secret thing'…I'm copying others as well, in a hope that we'll all welcome a change for the better.

Joe

She never responded back to me.

December 2007, A Glorious Day

Feeling alone…On this Glorious Day.

As I mask my emotions…And think of a way.

How shall I do it…Will anyone care?

What's it like…To be no longer there.

The love of my life…loves me no longer.

For years now…that thought I've pondered,

Our future uncertain…Each day I mature.

My birthday approaches…Will I see fifty-four?

What hurts me the most is…I love her so much.

She accepts no comfort…nor a warm touch.

So I exist in silence…on this Glorious Day.

Dabbing my tears…As I think of a way.

December 24, 2007

It's 8:15 pm as I write this. I'm home alone. About two weeks ago, as I was re-thinking Thanksgiving and wondering about Christmas—I really did try to see everyone's perspective. As often as I had thought that Yohan could visit her family anytime, but save holidays and occasions only if we're all invited…I got to thinking. Her fear would be losing the little bit of time and connections that she does have with them. I felt sorry for Yohan. She's almost in an awkward situation similar to how I feel. I had a change of heart. I don't mind if she spends all of the invited time with her family. And at this point, I don't really want to be invited anyway. I told all of this to Yohan and I felt good about it. But I still had that nagging question of: Why did they do this to me? So, my ex-step mother-in-law sent a Christmas card addressed to Yohan, our daughter and the dog. I was alone when I saw it, and I cried that someone could be so insensitive at Christmas time. I called the step-mother and then the half-sister…no answer at either line. When Yohan got home, I told her I'd tried to call. I tried again…no answer. So, I asked Yohan if I could make the call using her cell phone. She said NO. She said NO. She said NO. So, a short time later, I tried again and she answered.

I got very nervous, my voice was cracking, and I started to hyperventilate. I asked that she please speak with me for a few minutes and that Yohan was home and was aware that I was calling her. She said that she doesn't want to have this conversation, but that she would hear me out. I nervously spoke…probably for about 20 minutes. I mentioned that in the future we'll likely be at various family events together and that I wanted us to be able to speak comfortably and say hello. I don't want us to have to keep looking in the opposite direction. I said that it's not my intention to join them at Christmas, but my feelings were hurt when her Christmas card was received today. I reminded her that we shared coffee nearly every Sunday morning for 30 years. But every week our conversation consisted of just small talk. Neither we nor they ever shared personal business or happenings. Our relationship with them was never close. Consequently, there is no way that they would have known that the three-month separation that Yohan & I had was planned and we both agreed on it. (They thought that I just left her. And that is just so far from the truth.) So, I asked the step-mother to just please reconsider everything…just think it over, so that the next time we're in the same company we could all be a little more comfortable. She actually seemed okay with the conversation. My opinion was that we ended the conversation on a good note. All of this was about two weeks ago.

February 7th 2017

Wow…it's been 10 years since my last entry. But THIS one is my LAST entry. This has been on my mind since last October. Yohan and I were exhausted…had a long, busy day. We went to bed at about 9:00 pm. Shortly after getting into bed, I could almost swear that Yohan said I love you. (We had already kissed and said good night.) I was almost asleep, but I'm almost sure that's what she said (but I was facing the other way). I didn't respond. I was surprised. I didn't know what to say. Did I really hear that? Instead, it woke me up and I spent about two hours in thought. It took me several years to just accept that she doesn't love me…and now this. I don't know what to think. I know I don't feel loved. I haven't heard her say those words freely for years. At this point I feel like we've lost 15 years of our marriage which can never be recovered.

In a strange twist, last night we had just finished watching a show on TV (this is US). In this week's episode, the husband rented the couple's first apartment (which was vacant), for the evening…in order to surprise his wife. It brought tears to my eyes. I said to Yohan, "Familiar, isn't it?"

She said, "Yep."

Then went to bed shortly after. It's 10:30 now as I searched for this journal to scribble this final entry and review some of my previous writings. I think I want to include these entries in a book.

Additional Thoughts and Some Conclusions I've drawn

- When our kids were younger (about 12 and 7), one day, I showed them how to use the washer and drier, and we did a load of clothes. They were kind of excited to learn this. I suggested that maybe it would be good practice to do this every once in a while. Either way it's a good thing to know how to do this. When Yohan got home, I told her of this. Her response with teeth clenched, "I don't want them to ever do laundry," and she stormed off. I didn't think of it at the time, but…she was referring to the chores that she had to do every day. For a brief period, she allowed me to give them the responsibility taking turns at occasionally washing dishes, but she didn't support it so that barely lasted two or three weeks. I can't imagine her being so angry with me over such a minor 'offense.'

- One time, I recycled a piece of 'molded cardboard' (similar to molded cardboard as in an 'egg carton.' The cardboard had been sitting on the counter for a couple of weeks. When Yohan got home from work, I was next door visiting my neighbors. When she noticed the cardboard missing, she stormed into the neighbor's house (without knocking on the door) in a total rage…asking, "WHAT DID YOU DO WITH THAT CARDBOARD?"

I told her it went out in recycling.

She screamed, "DON'T TOUCH MY THINGS."

Then she stormed out the door.

Wow…what had just happened? About ten minutes later I returned home. She was burning. I told her that she owed our neighbors an apology for storming into their living room. And owed me an apology too…it was just cardboard. (Turned out that the cardboard held a 'food scale,' and she said that she kept the cardboard in case she transported the item back and forth to work.) She did apologize to the neighbors but didn't speak to me for days. She never apologized to me for such an outrageous outburst. And I know that she never will. She finds it very difficult to admit when she's wrong about something. From then forward, if for example, when I clean our bedroom, I do not dust her dresser or night-table…because I do not touch her 'things.' I can't imagine her being so angry with me over such a minor 'offense.'

- There was a time whereas in my family we were forced to have a discussion about child sexual abuse. (The conversations were not about me…instead it was about relatives.) With that said, at some point thereafter, she confided to me that she had a cousin who 'tried to do something with me' (her words). She told me who the cousin was. But she also insisted that nothing happened. Other than those few words, she refused to speak of it again…she refused to describe what happened or didn't happen. So, my thought is…is it possible that even if 'nothing happened,' could that experience alone have caused her trauma? Trauma that now after a major depression manifests itself in self-doubt and could include issues with intimacy? Even though we initially spoke of this incidence a few years ago, I couldn't help but to bring it up more recently, because I wondered if addressing it could help us. Yohan absolutely exploded and said that she was sorry that she even told me of it. So, we had no conversation about it.

- Since her natural mother died when Yohan was in the second grade, there was an immediate change in her daily routine. During that first year, she spent time with her mother's sisters (Aunts) and her cousins. She dearly missed her mother, but did enjoy time with relatives. When the step-mother and half-sister came into the mix the trauma of her mother's death and the future that betook her would affect her years later. She seemed to be level headed and content when we met and dated but even then she spoke of how her sister was the favorite and Yohan and her brothers were like pawns. (Typical Cinderella story.) Her brothers and their girlfriends/wives as well as we as a couple were never included in in that new family circle. We both surmised that her father needed a baby sitter, so he quickly dated then married and then secured the marriage with a child. I'd seen the step-mother in action…and yes, she certainly can be an 'evil step-mother.' Both of her brothers left that house as soon as they were 18. Both have failed marriages. One brother has multiple failed marriages…we're not sure how many times he was married. I understand that the 'trauma' that the three of them likely suffered can definitely manifest itself in negativity as one tries to understand, relate, and love. Even intimacy can suffer. I know first-hand how depression can cause you to delve deep into your sub-conscience evoking thoughts that cause you to even question your existence. I believe that Yohan suffered a severe depression as a result of her injury and the longevity of that injury. During this time, the trauma that she experienced as a child was brought to light in her mind. She'll never now be the same person that she was.

- After having read this book, you know that we participated weekly for about 10 years in 'county dancing.' This included line dances a well as couples dancing. But prior to that we spend about 10 years doing 'Polish Dancing.' So, we enjoyed dancing. However, in MY depression every little thing becomes the most important thing. At our son's wedding, I asked Yohan to dance with me, and she said no. Even now it's hard for me to say how much this hurt me…and just how important it was for me. At some point month/years later we were at a dinner/dance type of an event. Again, I asked her to dance…she said no. But shortly thereafter she accepted an offer from a business contact. I was hurt. Then at our daughter's wedding again she said no…so I joined a small crowd of others on the floor. Maybe she felt guilty, because a few minutes later she joined me. I know this sounds weird, but I can no longer ask her to dance with me. If she asks me, maybe I'll join. I know my depression is rooted in this somehow, but the rejection was just too powerful. I also can't initiate a hand-holding if we're walking…but I love it when she initiates it.

- Also, recently (2020), we went to bed, and I was feeling hopeful. I asked Yohan if it would be okay to snuggle against her and maybe touch her and kiss her neck. She had pajamas on, I didn't.
She hesitated then said, "I guess." So I fit into the curve of her back, put my hand around her waist, and kissed the back of her neck. My hand at her waist was touching her skin very slowly I inched my hand upward and touched her breast. At that instant her hand covered mine and she forcibly pulled my hand away from her.
I said, "You know you just pulled my hand off of you…why?"
Her reply was, "I don't know." And that was the end of that. So, what am I to think? Really, what am I to think? I'm totally confused.

- Rather recently (2021) I am just so starved to hear someone (my wife) say to me I love you, so I tried something…and this was extremely hard for me to do. Normally, as we would leave for work, we'd exchange a quick kiss, then just say, "Bye…have a good day."

So, one day as I was leaving first, I said "Have a good day Yohan, I love you."

It was as if she were a deer in my headlights. Her face was blank. It was an awkward moment, but she responded, "I love you." (She didn't say "too.")

Next day…same thing. Third day I said, "I love you." She didn't say anything. She just had a blank expression. I guess she was thinking, "What is he trying to do?" I guess it doesn't matter. The two times she did say it, it wasn't sincere. I give up. Actually, I suppose about three or four years ago, I really did just give up trying to win her affections back. I made a very conscious decision to just accept things as they are. I don't think she hates me, but I also know that she doesn't love me. Ages ago, when I asked her what does she want in me…? She said that she wanted me to be her companion. So, I guess I'm her companion. (I'd rather be her loving husband…but I'll have to accept being a companion.) I'll never again try to get her to talk about us…because I know she won't. I suppose it's a moot point.

- So…what is my absolute conclusion? I think Yohan is 'damaged goods.' She may have been damaged goods when we met…but neither of us knew it and I still am in love with her. As a result of everything that she has endured she may be damaged goods two or three times over. As a result of her being damaged goods. I TOO am now, damaged goods. I can't ask her to dance, I can't express my love, I can't clean her dresser, because I can't touch her 'things' (and our basement is filled with her 'things.' I know we'll never have sex again and I'm pretty sure that she'll never even touch me again. And I'll never get that long embrace or kiss. I'm probably damaged to the point that maybe even I couldn't have an intimate relationship due to zero confidence. Can you imagine being 46 years old and looking forward to the best part of your life…then by the time you're 47, the life you knew is over.

Sooo, Dementia/Alzheimer's runs in my family. As I write this sentence, I'm 67 years old. Dementia patients generally have a segment of time where they seem to only remember and reminisce about the past. If I'm stricken with it, I wonder if I'll go back in time to a segment when I knew I was loved. Maybe that will be the best part of my life.